TEACHING FOR SOCIAL JUSTICE?

TEACHING FOR SOCIAL JUSTICE?

VOICES FROM THE FRONT LINES

CONNIE E. NORTH

Paradigm Publishers
Boulder • London

Copyright © 2009 Paradigm Publishers

Published in the United States by Paradigm Publishers, 3360 Mitchell Lane, Suite E, Boulder, CO 80301 USA.

Paradigm Publishers is the trade name of Birkenkamp & Company, LLC, Dean Birkenkamp, President and Publisher.

North, Connie E.
  Teaching for social justice? : voices from the front lines / Connie E. North.
    p. cm.
  Includes bibliographical references and index.
  ISBN 978-1-59451-617-7 (hardcover : alk. paper)
  ISBN 978-1-59451-618-4 (paperback : alk. paper)
  1. Education—Social aspects—United States. 2. Teaching—Social aspects—United States. 3. Social justice—United States. I. Title.
  LC191.4.N67 2008
  370.11'5—dc22

                                                                                2008015128

Printed and bound in the United States of America on acid-free paper that meets the standards of the American National Standard for Permanence of Paper for Printed Library Materials.

Designed and typeset by Straight Creek Bookmakers.

13 12 11 10 09   1 2 3 4 5

Courage, it would seem, is nothing less than the power to overcome danger, misfortune, fear, injustice, while continuing to affirm inwardly that life with all its sorrows is good; that everything is meaningful even if in a sense beyond our understanding; and that there is always tomorrow.

—Dorothy Thompson

Contents

viii   *Contents*

Acknowledgments

Although words cannot adequately express my gratitude to those who made the completion of this book possible, I want to try to etch my appreciation here. This text simply would not be if it were not for the generosity of the four teachers in this study, whose bold and courageous voices told a story I felt compelled to write. Joe, your humility is stunning, and your attention to the connections among all living things continues to remind those of us lucky enough to know you what actually matters in our day-to-day lives. Julia, your articulate nuggets of wisdom always give me pause and belie your true age. Regardless of the classroom in which you land during the upcoming years, I have no doubt that your students will benefit from your thoughtfulness and dedication to their learning. Margaret, you became and remain a mentor to me. Witnessing your teaching talent firsthand was a gift. May your cup be emptied of frustration in the year to come and replenished with enough piss and vinegar to keep you in the teaching profession for the foreseeable future. Thanks also to your classroom mate, Vivian. Paul, although you might continue to fight an inner battle about where you teach, your commitment to meaningful, ethical, and democratic forms of education are unmistakable. By watching you, I learned just how invaluable the teaching and learning of theme-based, integrated curricula can be. Thanks also to Karen, your co-teacher.

I thank the Spencer Foundation for supporting my research and the school districts, principals, parents, and students who welcomed me into their schools. I also thank Dean Birkenkamp, Linda Carlson, Beth Davis, Dianne Ewing, Carol Smith, and Melanie Stafford at Paradigm Publishers for taking on this book and me and for your excellent guidance throughout the publishing process. Thanks also to Julia Cohen, Chris Myers, and Bill Pinar. Therese Quinn and Bill Ayers, I am grateful for your advice and thoughtful critiques. Your feedback motivated me to go forward with the publishing process.

Several university mentors also contributed mightily to the realization of the study and this book. Thanks to all who supported a research project that, in the eyes of many contemporaries, does not qualify as legitimate educational research. More specifically, Stacey Lee, your continued belief in my work as well as your expert advice enabled me to keep my chin up and my feet planted firmly in university soil. Simone Schweber, your bigheartedness, invaluable guidance and editing skills, and continuous support mean the world to me. May I someday be half the writer, mother, and human being that you are. Ken Zeichner, your dogged determination to make education (research) more democratic keeps my hope alive that a more just world and field are realizable. Thank you for allowing me to observe firsthand the value of university-school partnerships. Gloria Ladson-Billings, your teaching and research reveal that the term *activist-scholar* is not an oxymoron. Thank you for deepening my commitment to eliminating our educational debt. Diana Hess, thank you for expanding my notion of democracy, asking challenging questions, and modeling masterful teaching. Thank you also for sending me to Chicago. Harry Brighouse, thank you for continuing to push for the inclusion of philosophical questions into educational research and policymaking. If only I could acquire your charming disposition.

Additionally, Kevin Kumashiro, you and your scholarship give me hope that with some courage and eloquence, we can disrupt silence and invisibility. Thank you for your ongoing support and guidance. You, Jenny "Roach" Carney, and Shannon Kavanagh safeguarded my sanity in Chicago. On that score, thanks also to Stacey Horn, Erica Meiners, Therese Quinn, Stephen Russell, and Shannon Sullivan. Hilary Conklin, our work together greatly influenced my study methodology and reflection on it. Thank you for being an ethical researcher and supportive friend. Vonzell Agosto, your refusal to ask anything less than important, hard questions has greatly improved my work. I have no doubt that your verve will continue to inspire many, including me. Carl Grant, thank you for encouraging my scholarship and buying me coffee. Norris Court crew and related folks, especially Ben Aslinger, Wayne Au, Katie Elliott, Lia Ernst, Lauren Faulkner-Duncan, Ryan Flessner, Michelle Lavigne, Tori Maslow, Paula McAvoy, Shannon Reiter, and Jen Sandler, thank you for your ongoing encouragement and for providing much needed laughter throughout this project.

And beyond university walls ... PDS folks, particularly Mary Klehr and Ann Niedermeier, your wisdom about teaching and learning and dedication to bridging institutional gaps sustain my hope of creating substantive community-school-university partnerships. Constitutional Rights Foundation Chicago staff, thank you for pushing me to think more carefully about democratic literacy and bringing me into the fold of civic education. Richard Davis, your commitment to racial healing is rousing, your voice and music, a national treasure. Sid Heezen, I aspire to approach the world with your level of honesty and openness. Sarah Covington and Vivian Lin, thank you for your compassion, fantastic listening skills, and trips across the lake. I look forward to discovering where life takes us next. Kathleen P. and Larry Norris, you epitomize unconditional love. Simply put, thank you. Bill Fulton, when I doubt my ability to be the change I want to see, I think of you. Beth Binhammer, I am eternally indebted to you for guiding me to an "I" that is home, and one I want to inhabit at that. Thank you for sticking with me and embodying equanimity. Kristy Rogers, thank you for your sturdy shoulder, wisdom, and offerings of sanctuary during the volatile ups and downs of recent life transitions. You burst my world wide open and exposed me to myself, for which I will always be grateful.

Carey, Kelly, Dad, and Mom, although we might not share viewpoints when it comes to matters of social justice, I have known your love to be tried and true and your integrity to be unshakeable. Thank you for the thirty-two-plus years that you have invested in me.

Foreword

A few years ago, I wrote a newspaper article describing the disheartening trend of more and more inspiring and inspired teachers leaving the profession because of the barriers to teaching put into place with the current education "reforms." The narrow learning standards, scripted curriculum materials, high-stakes testing of students, and punitive uses of test results, along with the heightened demonization of public schools and public-school teachers made it difficult to keep alive the passion for creative and caring critical engagement in classrooms, especially for those teachers who recognize the inequities and diversities in schools and society and are trying to make a difference in the lives of their students. The situation has not improved. Around the world, nations are following suit, implementing standards-based reforms that mirror U.S. policies, despite compelling research by scholars such as Jean Anyon and Michael Apple that reveals the politically conservative originators of such reforms and the troublesome ways that resulting educational practices exacerbate inequities and, arguably, hinder our students' abilities to think critically and independently. The challenge for educators who are committed to social justice is daunting.

Yet, there is much reason for hope. Teaching for social justice happens not when the educational context is ideal, however that is defined or imagined, but rather, through working against the problems and paradoxes that mark any context. Such was the argument over thirty years ago by Paulo Freire and, more recently, by Carl Grant and Christine Sleeter, who each offer concrete suggestions for enacting multicultural education in this age of accountability and standardization. And such is the argument in this brilliant new book by Connie North. *Teaching for Social Justice?* offers a complex, insightful, and thorough fleshing out of what it means to teach for social justice in a conservative/neoliberal context by developing a framework of five "literacies," namely, functional, critical, relational, democratic, and visionary, that can be immeasurably useful for evaluating current work and imagining new possibilities. I found myself constantly thinking about my own classrooms, mapping various aspects of my teaching onto this framework and asking myself which literacies I seem to be advancing in different contexts and where I could be doing more. This book arrives at a time when it is sorely needed, a time when the political Left is struggling to define what we envision as "social justice" and how we can approach it through "teaching for social justice." Perhaps most useful is the concrete way that the framework puts into conversation a very broad and varied range of theoretical perspectives and, in doing so, models how the political Left—which is too often fractured—can speak across our differences as we build a more coordinated movement toward educational improvement.

Here in the concreteness of these ideas we learn from classroom teachers. The richly diverse group of four teachers in this study offers various models not only of what to do, but also of how to rethink the very practices in which we engage. Any practice is partial, has both strengths and weaknesses, and makes possible only certain kinds of learning and growth among our students, and thus the need to constantly trouble our own practices, our own visions, our own lenses. Indeed, this book grapples with the partialities of stories in a way that no other book that I have read has done by presenting multiple portraits of each person, or put another way, multiple versions of the same portrait that incorporate different sources of data, roles for researcher and participant, genres, and textual representations. There is not only one story to tell, or one analysis of that story, or one thing to learn from it. Different tellings and different readings invite different learnings—an insight that comes to life not only in these analyses of classrooms, but also in the classrooms themselves.

With this book, Connie North and her teacher colleagues have invited us to take a bolder step toward social justice. I look forward to seeing the changes that result.

—*Kevin K. Kumashiro*

Introduction

First they said I was too light
Then they said I was too dark
Then they said I was too different
Then they said I was too much the same
Then they said I was too young
Then they said I was too old
Then they said I was too interracial
Then they said I was too much a nationalist
Then they said I was too silly
Then they said I was too angry
Then they said I was too idealistic
Then they said I was too confusing altogether:
Make up your mind! They said. Are you militant
or sweet? Are you vegetarian or meat? Are you straight
or are you gay?

And I said, Hey! It's not about *my* mind.

—*June Jordan, "A Short Note"*

A wise educator (who not incidentally is the longtime partner of Paul, one of the teachers featured in this book) gave me invaluable advice when I set out on my research journey during the fall of 2006.[1] She said that university-based educational studies often do little more than expose the individual researcher's point of view on educational theories and phenomena. Researchers might deny that reality by using "scientifically valid" methods or claiming an "objective," "value-neutral" stance, but they end up speaking their subjective truths nonetheless. I want to begin this book by acknowledging explicitly that this is my story. Many people

1

and their ideas contributed mightily to it, and I suffused the following pages with the teachers' voices. Nevertheless, this book remains my take on a continuing inquiry into the significance and dilemmas of teaching for social justice. Like all human stories, it contains triumphs, failures, and missteps.

In the early stages of this project, an esteemed educational scholar spoke to a university audience about the need to conduct research for the public good. More specifically, she called for research that could shape macro-level educational policies. I remember her directly imparting a lesson to the crowd's novice researchers that she had learned over the course of her career as an educational scholar and activist. The gist of her message was that micro-level qualitative studies, like the one she completed for her doctorate, did nothing in Washington, D.C. As educators, we needed urgently and desperately to do something in our nation's capitol. "Leave your ethnographies behind, get out there, and influence state and federal policies," was the message I heard.

I also remember feeling deflated after leaving her talk. I had a long-standing desire and commitment to working with local educators, students, activists, and community members for the promotion of positive social change. I also loved to write. Was it impossible to realize larger-scale change through the written word? If so, why did novelists, poets, and playwrights continue to recognize and even celebrate the irony that "as one moves closer to the unique characteristics of a person or place, one discovers the universal" (Lawrence-Lightfoot and Davis 1997, 14)? In this *No Child Left Behind* society, was my intended path no longer a viable or useful one?

Questioning one's motives and assumptions is good, but a tipping point exists wherein doubt becomes crippling. Thankfully, I found people and texts that did not view education or social change as single-approach affairs. I particularly clung to Kevin Kumashiro's assertion that "every educational practice makes possible some antioppressive changes while closing off others" (2002, 9). I thus continued designing a research project that sought to make sense of all this talk about social justice by working with a small group of teachers in a single geographical area. But some unexpected things happened along the way, as they always do.

First and foremost, as I developed my research proposal, I fell in love with a woman. Simultaneously, the state in which I lived put to the vote a constitutional ban on same-sex marriage (and any institutionalized arrangement resembling marriage, such as civil unions). For me, a thirty-year-old white woman raised in the tree-lined upper-middle-class suburbs of Denver, Colorado, my decision to have a relationship with a woman quickly became more than a subjective matter. I tell you—the reader—this aspect of my personal life because my politicization around sexuality and gender identity issues influenced my thoughts about social justice and, thus, the claims about education for social justice that appear in this book. In reality, experiencing a strong dose of discomfort and discrimination on account of my sexuality has affected me in ways that extend far beyond what I rationally or consciously understand. But recognizing that my other privileges, especially those associated with my race and class, remain firmly entrenched and, even, that I can "cover" (Yoshino 2006) to guard many heterosexual privileges, have also assaulted my *psyche, soul, heart*—whichever terms you prefer.

Etched into this story, then, are deliberate and unconscious traces of my life's more recent and distant events. The intentional traces appear throughout the ensuing chapters as a way to remind you, the reader, that this text emerged from somewhere (Harding 1987). Indeed, through my writing, I am striving to unmask "the critical roles that language, social interactions, and pivotal experiences play in the production and transformation of subjectivity" (Bloom 1996, 178). At times, then, expect to see nontraditional forms of scholarly writing, including poems. These representations aim to make explicit the "ways in which the participants' voices are contextualized, the researcher's interpretations are partial, and the reader's reading is situated" (Kumashiro 2002, 20).

My judgments and blind spots inevitably entered into both the research process and creation of this text. Rather than viewing these inadvertent biases as blemishes on my work, I see them as opportunities to remember that unconscious fears and desires are an inescapable part of the human experience. As June Jordan (1980) reminds us, we are all confusing and full of contradictions. Happily, our interactions with others can expose harmful prejudices, granting us the opportunity to work through them (Wilson 2002). I thus invite your feedback on my incomplete reading of the world. Perhaps your engagement with this book will bring your own hidden assumptions to light. I welcome that effect, too, as I am trying to use story as analysis—to evoke in addition to represent, to generalize through the resonance of readers, and to open up rather than close down conversation (Ellis 2004, 22).

Why Study *Social Justice* with Teachers?

These days, educational researchers, administrators, and policymakers frequently use (or refuse to use) *social justice* without offering an explanation or defense of its social, cultural, economic, and political significance. The benign or intentional failure to define this decidedly undecided term threatens to evacuate social justice of meaning and, more importantly, power. Moreover, the people most directly impacted by the policies and practices designed and executed under the banner of social justice—namely, teachers, students, and parents—are oftentimes missing from the decision-making table. Their absence undermines the importance of *democracy,* too.

This book addresses these issues by bringing the voices of four K–12 educators into the university-centered debates on social justice. More specifically, it documents our five-person study group's exploration of the meanings of social justice and the applications of its principles in the teachers' classrooms and communities. My portrayal of this collective journey aspires to advance discussions about the possibilities and limitations of employing particular strategies for social justice education in particular institutional settings. As such, this book challenges the efficacy and desirability of implementing top-down, one-size-fits-all policy proposals that neglect the significant influence of local historical, political, sociocultural, and economic factors. Given the study's focus on collaborative inquiry *with* teachers, it also deepens the connections between theory and practice.

Despite the strengthened institutional and ideological barriers to making schools sites of social transformation at the dawning of the twenty-first century (Anyon 2005; Apple 2001), many teachers are trying to make a difference. Public discussions about their situated practices and philosophies can simultaneously inspire hope for carrying out transgressive education and paint a realistic picture of what is possible within the constraints of our existing social order and its schools. By bringing together this group of teachers on a monthly basis both to dialogue about social justice issues and to observe each other's teaching, this project sought to create a forum where educators could affirm, reinforce, challenge, and transform our philosophies on and approaches to education for social justice. I owe a great debt to the teachers who opened their classrooms, hearts, and minds to this study. Without them, this book would not exist.

Roadmap

In the following pages, I alternate between telling the teachers' individual stories and situating those narratives in a larger context. More specifically, I juxtapose each teacher's perspective and practice with both our study group dialogues and scholarship on education for social justice. My analysis is organized around five competencies that emerged as the foci of the teachers' instruction over the course of the study: functional, critical, relational, democratic, and visionary literacies. Importantly, *literacy* in this book is not limited to learning how to read and write. Rather, the five literacies described herein refer to the competencies students need both to excel at schooling (or at least successfully manage it) and to effect positive change at local and more global levels. Also notable are the individual teachers' varied commitments to each competency as a result of their diverse beliefs, educational contexts, and encounters with institutionalized oppression, domination, and privilege. A significant part of this story involves exposing the contested nature of these five literacies in struggles for social justice as well as the specific teacher and institutional factors that shaped and constrained students' cultivation of them.

The first chapter introduces Margaret, a white, veteran seventh-grade language arts teacher at a small, urban, charter middle school, where most students are African-American, Latino, and Hmong and qualify for free or reduced lunch. Her teaching illustrates the importance of functional literacy in education for social justice as well as the limitations of focusing one's instruction on it, both of which I take up in chapter two. Briefly, cultivating functional literacy involves teaching students to "succeed academically in the traditional sense" (Gutstein 2006, 30). The cultivation of functional literacy in mathematics, for example, enables students to "achieve on standardized tests, pass high school, succeed in college, have access to advanced mathematics courses, and pursue (if they choose) mathematics-related careers" (Gutstein 2006, 30). The significance of functional literacy to social justice is most evident in cases where students do not arrive at the schoolhouse door with ample academic knowledge and skills, as was the case in Margaret's classroom.

In chapter three, the reader meets Joe, an American Indian and Filipino teacher of high school social studies and art. When the study began, he was in his eighth year of teaching at a small, alternative city public school with a strong anti-oppressive mission. His teaching emphasized critical literacy. Unlike functional literacy, critical literacy seeks to confront the unjust elements of the status quo through the development of critical consciousness (Gutstein 2006). Accordingly, instead of emphasizing increased access to academic opportunities, as functional literacy does, critical literacy seeks to challenge "the structures and inequitable relations of power that created an access issue in the first place" (Gutstein 2006, 30). My analysis of critical literacy in chapter four addresses the strengths of Joe's instructional approach as well as the unintended negative consequences of his inattention to functional literacy.

Chapter five presents Julia, a white Jewish lesbian who was also the youngest, least experienced teacher study participant and the only teacher working in a more rural district, located approximately ten miles from the city center. When the study began in January 2006, Julia was a coordinator of the Reach Program, a program created for academically struggling students at Hancock High School. During the second half of the study, she taught eighth-grade mathematics at Hancock Middle School. Julia's teaching highlights the importance of relational literacy and its sometimes-conflicting relationship with functional and critical literacies. At its crux, relational literacy involves meeting human beings' fundamental need to be cared for (Max-Neef, Elizalde, and Hopenhayn 1991). My exploration of relational literacy seeks to bring caring into discussions of education for social justice and, more specifically, solidarity. It also qualifies "caring" because paternalistic, artificial forms of it frequently harm rather than help students (Antrop-González and De Jesús 2006; Popkewitz 1998; Valenzuela 1999). I elaborate on relational literacy and the issues accompanying its development in chapter six.

Chapter seven depicts Paul, a white veteran co-teacher of eleven-to fourteen-year-olds in a small K–8 private school. His school emphasizes "progressive education," which it defined as "creating an environment in which children's strengths and unique ways of learning are supported." Paul's teaching illuminates the significance of democratic literacy and the contextual factors contributing to the successful teaching of it. Democratic literacy resembles relational literacy with its focus on interpersonal interactions. However, it also emphasizes public interactions with strangers (Parker 2006) that promote mutual understanding and informed decision making on issues impacting the common good. Chapter eight focuses on the benefits of intentionally developing democratic literacy in the classroom as well as the potential dangers of practicing democratic skills in a society that has deeply entrenched social inequalities. I use an impromptu discussion about illegal immigration that occurred in

Julia's classroom to emphasize the care with which democratic literacy must be cultivated in U.S. educational settings that aspire to realize social justice.

The book concludes with an appeal to educators, scholars, and policy-makers to recognize the value of visionary literacy in struggles for social justice. As the spoken word movement illustrates, visions of a more just future are frequently cultivated via visual and performing arts. Accordingly, teaching that focuses narrowly on enhancing students' technical skills too often curtails opportunities for productive imaginings. Drawing on the teachers' promotion of visionary literacy, I argue that actively imagining better personal and collective stories gives students hope. As such, visionary literacy engenders and sustains students' and teachers' commitment to engaging "the world as agents of change" (Stovall 2006, 64). The subsequent, concluding chapter focuses on how the study group members sustain our own visions of an improved world. It also examines the contribution of this study to the realization of education for social justice. In short, the tail end of this story emphasizes that "[w]here oppression or exploitation or pollution or even pestilence is perceived as natural, as a given, there can be no freedom. Where people cannot name alternatives or imagine a better state of things, they are likely to remain anchored or submerged" (Greene 1995, 52).

PART I

FUNCTIONAL LITERACY

1

Functional Literacy in Context

A Portrait of Margaret

(Margaret's responses to the portrait appear in italics.)
"Alright, folks, I need your attention," Margaret said in a tone and at a volume impossible to ignore. Although petite, this silver-haired woman, who always wore glasses and never lipstick, was a force to be reckoned with. The seventh graders returned to their respective desks, lined up in rows, and with undeveloped slyness continued to exchange insults with their peers, stab each other with pencils, or give unsuspecting friends a smack upside the head. Margaret saw all of these actions and glared at each of the perpetrators in turn until all eyes were on her and all hands rested immobile on top of or below the desks. "You guys are so not smooth," she joked.

The wall by the door held some framed landscape artwork and, more notably, a large bulletin board covered with photographs of students from previous years. Margaret clustered the photos by year and included quotes from the pictured students, like, "These kids ain't bad; they just got issues." Windows overlooking a busy four-lane street ran along the back of the room, where Margaret and Vivian, the special education teacher with whom she shared her classroom, each had a corner nook to house their desks and personal belongings. The wall between the chalkboard and windows displayed student work and "magic words," the first item on this day's agenda, which Margaret had written on the chalkboard at the front of the classroom.

"Monique, pick a magic word and use it in a sentence," Margaret instructed while grabbing the raffle tickets and a glass jar off her desk.

"Middle school students are accustomed to having homework," a student with piercing green eyes said in a matter-of-fact way.

"That'll work," Margaret said as she handed her a ticket. Monique wrote her name on it, and Margaret placed it in the jar. On the first day of the next month, Margaret would randomly draw a ticket and reward the winning student with five dollars.

"Alright, so accustom is off the table. Darius, you're up," Margaret said, ignoring the handful of students who were bouncing up and down with their arms raised.

"I concealed my magic word ticket so Daniel wouldn't steal it," a tall, lanky student mumbled into his crossed arms that rested on the desk.

"Darius, honey, nobody heard that. Say your sentence loudly and clearly."

"I CONCEALED MY MAGIC WORD TICKET SO DANIEL WOULDN'T STEAL IT," Darius boomed.

"Smart move, Darius. Here's your ticket. Ricardo, *cómo se dice,* 'I said the magic word,' *en español*?" Margaret asked.

"*Yo dije la palabra mágica,*" a student with stylishly spiked hair replied.

"*Yo dije la palabra mágica,*" Margaret repeated. "Thank you, Ricardo, for the Spanish tutorial." As she deposited a ticket on his desk, Margaret turned to a sullen female student. "Tonisha, can you say, '*Yo dije la palabra mágica*'?"

"No," replied Tonisha. She sulked, flipped her long, neat braids, and slumped down in her chair.

"Ah, come on and try it. Just humor me for a moment. Curtis, you up for the challenge?"

"*Yo dije la palabra mágica,*" fumbled the class clown, casting a smile that lit up the room.

"Excellent effort. That merits a ticket." Turning her attention to the back corner of the classroom, Margaret said, "What are you drawing over there, Chris?" as she approached his desk. "Nice work. I love confiscating things I like." Margaret snatched up the piece of paper in front of Chris. "Give me a reason why I should give this masterpiece back to you at the end of class by using a magic word."

Chris used his bright coffee-colored eyes to glare at Margaret but said in a voice that all his classmates could hear, "I toiled on that picture, which isn't finished."

"Here you are, sir." Margaret placed a ticket in front of him, and Chris began doodling on it as soon as it hit the table.

"We have three native Spanish speakers in here, so we should make good use of their services, as knowing a second language is valuable and very cool," Margaret said. "I encourage you to spend time practicing your Spanish. If we had a native Hmong speaker in this class, I would encourage us to learn how to say things in Hmong as well. Now, who wants to run the show for the last seven tickets?"

"I do," a female student with a mouthful of braces replied. She leaped out of her chair, extending an open hand. Margaret placed the tickets in it and moved to the opposite side of the room.

"Sheila, I need to hear everything that happens so speak in a loud, clear voice and ask the other students to do so as well."

Sheila called on a student with pale blue eyes, who said in a soft voice, "Eating vegetables is beneficial to my health."

"What did you say?" Sheila barked.

"Sheila," Margaret admonished, "saying 'what?' like Crystal is stupid is the wrong thing to do when you are in charge of a task. You need to adjust your tone and ask her, in a respectful way, to repeat the sentence."

"What did you say, Crystal?" Sheila said with sugar in her voice. I made eye contact with Margaret, who shook her head in amusement. Crystal repeated her sentence so that at least Sheila could hear it, and Sheila subsequently distributed the remaining tickets to her peers without interference from Margaret.

"Alright, it's time to work on making inferences, which is a fancy way of saying we're going to solve problems using information that we already have. You need your language arts folder, your notebook, and something to write with."

Several students yelled out, "I need a pencil, Ms. Nowak."

Margaret retrieved several pencils from her desk and, as she passed them out, declared, "If you need to sharpen your pencils, do it now, because I don't want to be interrupted once we start this activity."

Finding Ms. Nowak

I met Margaret while tutoring in her seventh-grade language arts classroom at Johnson Middle School during the fall of 2005. The idea of recruiting Margaret as a study participant emerged after watching her teach during my initial months of tutoring. The decision to ask her to be part of the study, however, occurred after I had already begun it. I was interviewing one of the other teacher participants, Joe, in mid-January when I realized how valuable Margaret's voice would be to the study group.

"I've been talking a lot with this teacher I'm tutoring for at Johnson who has a lot of African-American students," I said to Joe as we talked about the lack of teachers of color in the United States and, more generally, the inability of many teachers to be effective with students who are not white and/or middle class. "She's a white woman," I continued, "and when she teaches, she really seems to command her students' respect. She sets clear boundaries for them and is always explicit about both her purpose for doing something and her expectations of the students. She sets high but realizable goals for them, making her classroom a safe space where students don't feel demoralized. I think because she has garnered their respect, they're responsive and she has been able to conquer part of the alienation that so many black students experience in schools. Being in her classroom has made me think a lot about the relationship between kids feeling disrespected and many of the discipline problems that teachers face."

"Yeah, this issue of respect would be a good study in and of itself."

"I wish Margaret were in the study because she's been teaching middle school language arts for a number of years and—"

"Did you ask her?" Joe interjected.

"I didn't." I sighed. "It's been recently occurring to me that I should. I don't know if Margaret would identify herself as teaching for social justice, but I think she models Lisa Delpit's philosophy. Have you read *Other People's Children*?"[1]

"No, I've seen it, but—"

"She talks a lot about the tension between honoring students' cultural backgrounds and teaching them the skills they need to gain access to the system so they can change the status quo. Delpit argues for tackling institutionalized racism and other forms of oppression but, at the same time, wants teachers to acknowledge that a code of power exists, and students need access to the rules of this code if they are going to be able to challenge it successfully.

Over the years, I have developed what appears to be an unhealthy disregard for academic scholarship regarding education issues. I had never heard of this woman, or her book, until I met Connie. If that is what Lisa Delpit said, I certainly agree with her. However, is she in a classroom putting her knowledge to some use? How many teachers have changed their practice because of her book? I am reminded of what Joe said at our August 2006 meeting. No matter how many times he heard something from his teachers, he needed to experience life for himself before he could make the kinds of changes that led him out of dead-end jobs and on to a successful career as an artist and teacher. Some people (probably including me) need to find everything out the hard way. I don't know that reading Delpit's book would have made any difference in my teaching.

"This is the kind of teaching that I think Margaret does," I said. "She helps students develop a lot of skills, but she will tell them directly, 'I'm not having you learn these skills for learning's sake alone. I'm having you learn them because they're going to be important for you to know when you want to get access to certain things as adults.'"

"Does she use those terms with her students?" Joe asked.

"She does," I replied with conviction.

"If her students understand that that's what she's doing, I would imagine they respond well to her teaching."

"Watching her at work, I am always impressed with how often she is explicit with her students about why she is teaching a lesson in a certain way. She scaffolds her lessons beautifully and will say things like, 'I don't expect you all to know these skills already.'"

"Good for her," Joe said. "Wow. Now that's a skill I would like to develop."

"Maybe I can get her to be in the study after all," I said, laughing. "I think it would make this study more meaningful to have a classroom teacher in the group who works in a school with such an ethnically, racially, and socioeconomically mixed group of kids."

A Short History of Johnson Middle School

"So Johnson Middle School was created in 1994?" I asked Margaret while interviewing her in her living room on a cold February evening.

"1993," Margaret corrected. "It opened as a charter school on the east side of town in a building that served as a temporary space to launch the school. I took a language arts job there in '95. I wanted to get out of ESL, and this position was a shot."

"I know the school moved to the north side in 1997. Did the student population change when the school moved sites?"

"The second or third year that we moved to the new building, I had my class do a project on the history of our school," Margaret said. "Although the city's demographics are rapidly changing, and these changes are making Hobson less white, Johnson remains one of the few schools in town with a racially and ethnically diverse student population. I had the students go back and interview the original principals, teachers, and kids who had been at the first building. One of the things that we did was pull demographic data on the student population from the time the school opened. I remember we made a line graph, and it sort of went like this." Margaret created a large *X* in the air with her index fingers.

"The year that we moved to our current location, it jumped one hundred eighty degrees," Margaret continued, shaking her head. "It was so stunning. The students' racial and ethnic backgrounds completely flipped overnight. The politics of the funding, staffing, and population of that school is intriguing for anybody who is interested in the racial politics of Hobson." Margaret paused. "It was not an experience, believe me, that I ever would have chosen to live through. Had I known what was coming, I would have gotten a job as a manager at Wal-Mart and just been done with it." I laughed at the improbable image of Margaret bowing to Sam Walton's heirs.

"But, you know, it's like any other experience," Margaret said. "Once you're in it, if you manage to come out in one piece on the other side, you're a smarter and richer person for it. Although it's not the kind of thing that anybody would knowingly subject herself to, unless you're a masochist. It was," Margaret paused again. "It was really a brutal transition."

"Well, the old building is tucked back in the wealthy, white, overeducated hills of the east side, isn't it?" I asked.

Margaret nodded. "And when the charter school was in that location, the student population reflected that. But right before we moved to the new location, which is a predominantly African-American area, our black principal was fired. That decision created a nasty situation because the district pulled a white guy out of retirement to replace him. This was a huge mistake and only exacerbated the racial tensions that the former principal had already fueled. The black community on the north side hated us—the principal and the teachers—because we were all white. And the students, well I'm not sure what the agenda was downtown. Several kids that the district office sent to Johnson had already been expelled from other schools.

"It's a funny process to go through," Margaret continued. "To realize what it feels like when somebody is specifically and deliberately out to get you because of your race. It doesn't matter what really happened or who you are. The only thing that matters is your skin color. To have experienced it once to the extent that I did is a fairly unique experience for a white woman of my generation and social class who wasn't looking for it. I didn't, say, go to Selma, Alabama, in 1963. I wasn't knowingly putting myself in harm's way for a higher cause. All I wanted was a job," Margaret said, laughing. "I was so clueless about what I was getting myself into."

"So what changed the dynamics at the school?" I asked.

"Well, they hired a new African-American principal, Mike. Looking back on it, I don't think the board of education had any choice except to hire him. Mike was exactly the right person at the right time for that school. He was the community's choice for principal and created enough social and political stability to let the situation settle into a place where the staff could at least get our footing. I don't think there are many people who could have come in and done what he did."

Margaret's Path to Teaching

"When I was in seventh grade, we moved to New Jersey from Chicago because my father was transferred," Margaret said as she leaned into her chocolate leather sofa. "I went to high school in what was basically an affluent suburb of New York City. It was a very homogenous school. Everybody was white, and everybody was in the middle to upper-middle class. The major identifiable ethnic groups were Italians and Jews. There was one black family in our entire town, whom I never knew."

"Did you go straight to college after graduation or—"

"I did, but I crashed and burned that first year of college—flunked my first class, went home for a year, and came back. I really don't like school. I know that sounds odd coming from a teacher, but I don't like being a student or doing the kinds of things students have to do. I find them really confining and boring. I think at the tail end of my high school years, I realized that nothing really bad was going to happen to me if I refused to study or do my homework. You understand that this was the time of the Vietnam protests and women's movement. Everybody was protesting everything. I thought, well why study for tests that I don't care about or write papers on subjects that don't interest me? So I quit. That experience really influenced my attitude about encouraging kids to go to college. I went to college because nobody ever told me that there was anything else I could do. There were no choices. Nobody asked, 'Who are you? What do you want? What are your goals?'"

"So you went home for a year and then came back, but you didn't finish. Did you do something else for a while?"

"Well, yeah, that was the misspent youth I've alluded to. Hating school wasn't the only thing that was happening in my life," Margaret said. "I dropped out of class. I dropped out of a lot of stuff. I was sort of like a tourist in the underbelly of American society. If you're born and raised in a middle-class environment, you can never really be poor. But you can have no money and know a whole lot of other people who come from much lower social and economic circumstances than you do. Even though you are a visitor in that world, you get a pretty good, up close and personal look at what that life is like. When you're a university student and don't have any money, that's genteel poverty; I was an adult for real with no money and no prospects, working at really crummy jobs. It's hard to know which job I had that was the worst. I was a temp, maid, grocery store cashier, uniform store clerk. Oh my God, that was just a surreally grotesque job!

"The reason I even got into teaching was because I passed the Hobson Literacy Council every day on my way to work as a legal secretary. I had just seen a TV documentary about illiteracy among adults and was stunned that there were adults who couldn't read. It never crossed my mind. You can know people and interact with them for a long time, but do it in circumstances that don't expose their lack of literacy skills.

"So I stopped in at the literacy center to volunteer and was trained as a literacy tutor. Tutoring was the first thing that I ever really liked doing in my life. They had two tutoring programs, one for ESL tutees. For some reason, I decided that tutoring ESL would be a really good idea and eventually wound up being a trainer for the literacy council. I tacked on an ESL certification when I went back to school because somebody, at some point, told me that if I had it, it would be easier to get a job. This was really good advice. The only reason the school district hired me in 1989 was because I had ESL certification. They didn't need English teachers then anymore than they do now."

Teaching with Socratic Circles

Sometimes
during the course
of five classes a day,
I see at least one of just about everything:

English speakers Spanish speakers Hmong speakers
"Other" speakers;
kids who identify themselves as
    white,
       black,
          mixed,
             Asian,
                Mexican,
                    Native American,
                        African-American.
Kids from families that are rich, poor, and middle class.

A-students, F-students and everything-in-between students.
Kids who are outgoing, shy, happy, depressed,
curious, bored, boring, mean, kind, awkward, confident,
mature, articulate, and tongue-tied—
sometimes all in the same class period.

Kids who sometimes can't sit still and
kids who sometimes can't stay awake;
kids who hate school,
kids for whom school is a refuge,
kids who figure they might as well
be in school as anywhere else.

I see them in groups of fifteen to twenty,
for fifty minutes
whether I'm at my best
or my worst
or somewhere in between,
whether *I* feel like it or not,
and whether *they* feel like it or not.

So wrote Margaret (although not in poetic stanzas) in her paper on Socratic Circles for the classroom action research project in which she and

five other Johnson teachers participated. This yearlong individual and collaborative process involved examining and improving literacy across content areas. Being present as Margaret both implemented and evaluated this instructional strategy gave me much insight into her views on student learning, effective teaching, and power relations.

At first glance, Socratic Circles seem like a simple instructional strategy. Margaret posted a student's definition of Socratic Circles in her classroom because he captured so well the central objective of this method: "Socratic Circles are teaching circles where we use questions to help each other learn." To run Socratic Circles, the teacher selects a text for students to read, and the students individually write questions based on their readings of the text. The students then divide into an inner and outer circle: The inner circle is responsible for discussing the text, and the outer circle evaluates the quality of the inner circle's conversation. The teacher or a student can kick off the discussion with a focal question about the text and, ideally, all the students in the inner circle subsequently engage in a meaningful conversation with each other, as the outer circle and teacher observe. The teacher only intervenes when the students need more information or the discussion has gone awry. As Margaret wrote, "If the students are well prepared, the teacher should be almost unnecessary."

The preparation for a Socratic Circle is what makes it an intensive, multifaceted enterprise. Unlike some schools, wherein student-centered discussions are the norm rather than the exception, Margaret teaches in a building where most classrooms have straight rows of desks facing the front of the room. According to Margaret, there are two intentional reasons for this architecture: "Classrooms are designed to be efficient ways for one person to deliver information to a large group of people who are there for the purpose of hearing what the information giver has to say," and the "standard middle school classroom arrangement model ... is a hierarchical system designed to visually establish and reinforce a teacher's power." By introducing a circular seating arrangement and ceding her power to the students during Socratic Circles, Margaret challenged the entrenched view of acceptable classroom activities. She therefore had to invest significant time and energy in preparing the students to take greater responsibility for both their learning and behavior.

Margaret decided the students would have to master seven social and intellectual skills if they were going to participate in successful Socratic Circles:

1. Take turns civilly and equally
2. Ask questions
3. Be responsible for their own behavior
4. Speak loudly enough for everyone to hear
5. Redirect or reinvigorate a stalled conversational line
6. Monitor their own comprehension
7. Understand and apply the rules for public, formal discussions

In strategizing how her students could best learn these skills, Margaret considered what her students were already bringing to the circle. That is, she did not assume that they were starting from ground zero. Recognizing that her students were connoisseurs of informal conversations but needed to learn the norms of public, formal discussions, she wrote, "[It] was time to teach my students the rules of the game I actually wanted them to play."

Margaret therefore refined the list of skills and knowledge that her students would need in order to "take over her job":

1. Know how to ask questions
2. Know the language for interrupting, disagreeing, and agreeing
3. Know how to present themselves physically: eye contact, posture, voice quality
4. Understand the difference between formal and informal discussions and identify examples of each
5. Understand the social significance of using one discussion style over another
6. Believe in each other as reliable sources of information
7. Believe that it is important to know this stuff

From this list, she developed mini-lectures and activities to help students understand how to participate "in a learning community of their peers" and conduct public, formal discussions that by and large rely on middle-class "codes of behavior" (Pattillo 2007). For example, she drew on Doug Buehl's (2001) work to help her students understand the difference between two types of questions: thin questions, which clarify meaning and vocabulary and usually have straightforward, simple answers, and thick questions, which move a discussion forward and engage others. By using the terms *thin* and *thick,* Margaret sought to give her students "a way to identify the function the questions serve and, thereby, help them organize their discussion."

When the students finally undertook their first Socratic Circles, Margaret was pleased with the students' ability to conduct an independent discussion on an article that addressed the single-sex schools debate. Although the kids initially reacted with reckless abandon to the new arrangement of classroom space—a pile of pillows in the middle of a room and a ring of chairs surrounding it—many students asked interesting questions and stepped into leadership roles during the discussion, without Margaret's guidance. As Margaret wrote, "To my very great pleasure, several students noted that it was fun to talk to their peers without the intermediary of a teacher." Additionally, the students in the outer circle solemnly filled out the evaluation form Margaret had created and made astute observations about the content and quality of their peers' discussion. Emphasizing the importance of student feedback, she wrote,

> I cannot teach these skills without the Outer Circle. If you skip that step, the whole experience is diminished. Kids like to be observers [and are] capable of making use of the information they receive from their observations. You can't watch yourself, but you can watch people like you (i.e., your fellow seventh-grade classmates) and see yourself in what they do.

In their evaluations of the first Socratic Circles, Margaret also saw the students acknowledge that the discussion skills they had learned held long-term value. As one of her students wrote, "I think I will need Socratic Circle information in the future." Moreover, Margaret was impressed by the students' ability to regulate their own and others' behavior to further group interactions. In Margaret's eloquent words,

> It seems that when the social behaviors are (1) explicitly taught, and (2) the guidelines for using them are clear, and (3) they are in a situation where *they* are responsible for the way they act (e.g., Socratic Circles), the kids will follow through. When they have the language, they can name the behavior and talk about it; they will cue each other about how to act. I have spent many hours telling children to sit up straight, make eye contact, etc. etc. etc. This year was the first time I can recall one seventh grader telling another one to sit up straight and look at them when they were talking to them. Removing myself from the interaction was the only way to create

a situation where failure to make eye contact was a breach of etiquette between peers and not a way to defy authority (emphasis original).

Ultimately, Margaret felt that the Socratic Circle allowed students to take conversations in intellectual directions that interested them. As she wrote, "Even though I chose the topic, none of the conversations developed the way they would have if I had been leading the discussion." This finding, as well as the students' overzealous response to the new seating arrangement, introduced questions for Margaret that invigorated her desire to keep growing and learning as a teacher. Although Margaret ended her research paper by noting that many of the possibilities revealed by Socratic Circles remained unexplored, she accomplished one of her primary goals through the use of this instructional strategy: "a transfer of power" via "the transfer of the responsibilities attendant on that power and the skills necessary to execute those responsibilities."

Margaret's Philosophy of Teaching: A Soliloquy

Setting the scene: It is now 8:30 p.m., and Connie has been interviewing Margaret for approximately ninety minutes. Margaret is on a roll and impassionedly describing her theories of teaching and learning with little interference from Connie. Hence the soliloquy that appears below.

"If you look at schools for what they really are, they sort of make sense. After all, what are you gonna do with a whole bunch of kids under eighteen? They've got to be somewhere, and they're not good for a whole lot of stuff in a society like ours. On balance, they might as well spend the day with me. I'm a nice person, and I like children. Many people don't get that public education is a foundation of America. Without public education, the country would fall apart. I'm sure some people would say I am doing a *Reader's Digest* version of the holy teacher rosary, but without schools, we would have no way of delivering the many social and health services that are currently fed through our school system. Teachers are very fond of saying that these services detract from our mission of education, and I used to believe that. But now I have a more global view of the function of public education. Except for the very rich and social outcasts, it's the one unifying factor that Americans have. We don't have a draft anymore, and even that only hit men.

"School is sometimes the only safe place where a child is all day long. Why isn't that at least as important as where to put an apostrophe? How can you say, 'The fact that I come to this building every day and am a stable, loving role model in a safe environment for a vulnerable child is detracting from the time I could spend teaching where to put punctuation marks in a paragraph'? Doesn't that just sound demented? What is my job? Why does somebody pay me fifty thousand dollars a year to show up in my classroom every day? Quite honestly, I don't think it is to teach my students about punctuation. It's my job to train my students to take their place in a society that they need to be ready for. Having not only navigated the system myself but also having taken a few really nasty and nonproductive detours, I have had a chance to see what kinds of things have mattered to me in my life and which haven't, what has held me back and what has helped me succeed. I think a lot about my unfortunate years as a twenty-something-year-old and all of the people who I will never see again because they will never make it up and out to the place where I am. I think a lot about the difference between them and me. The one thing that I have always come back to is that this difference is absolutely not about intelligence.

"We've sort of perverted the idea of education with all this talk of credentials, and I see the idea passed on to kids that all they need is a piece of paper. I did foster care for ten years and shepherded several children through high school, which was not about education. It was about getting that damn piece of paper so you could show it to someone. It's like the whole program is about students turning themselves into the person that teachers want them to be. We say, 'Well, we're the role model. If you're not like me, then apparently you're just not worth anything.' I find that really offensive and soul-sucking—it's the kind of thing that destroys children. And we wonder why they drop out when they're fifteen?

"I see the delusion about adulthood in middle school and the absolute terror in seventeen- and eighteen-year-old kids who are facing an adult life that they are ill prepared for. They are absolutely convinced that if they cannot write well, don't know U.S. history, don't read literature, or cannot do a science experiment that the adult world has no place for them. *Yet, there are many types of jobs in our society for people who do not have these skills. They are not necessarily places of high status or upward mobility. However, they are places where people can make a living.* Our idea of helping them is to work them to death or offer them some kind of aid program that's gonna help them be the kind of person that we're comfortable with *[i.e., a college graduate]* because we're just not comfortable with anything except lawyers in our *[many educators']* version of life.

"We talk about being sensitive to diversity, yet we only welcome diversity that fits whatever it is that we teach at school, which often focuses on taking notes, being neat and organized, and showing up on time. *All too often, our agenda rewards these (our) skills and devalues the students' own strengths and talents. And when we do pay attention to their unique abilities, what do we do with that information? Kids with a talent for working with their hands are not usually channeled into skilled trades. Students with a talent for working with people are not often encouraged to open a nail salon or be a hairdresser. Whatever skills or talents we discover in them are immediately translated into a college major.* Take a look at school. What the hell do we value?

"The people in school buildings are not bad people. They're usually really nice adults who have devoted their lives to working with children. They love kids, and they see that some of these kids are living in poverty and, sometimes, misery. They don't want them to suffer, have babies at fifteen, and live on the street. But in the many little things that teachers say and do, they often don't pay attention to who these kids are. I try very, very hard to listen to my kids. I mean really listen to them. Not like, 'I heard what you said,' but rather, 'If this is who you are and this is what you believe, then as your teacher, that must mean I need to do this for you instead of that.' I think that one of my strengths as a teacher is being willing to do what my kids need and not what I want. I feel deeply that to have a life that is meaningful—to have some integrity—you have to connect with who you really are. This is a foundational piece of who I think I am in the classroom. I can't help my students with everything because I am not their mother and can't teach them how to operate in their social sphere or community. But I try to meet them in that place where what they need and what I can give them connect.

"When you get at the core of what I'm trying to teach them to do, the content is completely secondary. That's why I would say I don't care what I teach. I'd teach anything and did as an ESL teacher. Content doesn't matter to me because the thrill is not in delivering content; it's in teaching children. I think for a lot of teachers at the middle and high school levels that's lost. Maybe you get that at the elementary school level, that pure love of teaching because there is not an obsession with first-grade literature. Mostly, I think they just love kids. They love teaching them, nurturing them, watching them grow, and helping them develop skills. But somehow by middle school, it becomes all about content. It's all about the teacher, not the kids.

"Now some teachers love kids but also want the kids to love them. I've avoided that trap. Pick an inspirational poster with a sunset on it, but the less you care about whether or not the kids like you, the more they'll respond to you. I actually become a little more likable each year because I'm a role model for failure rather than perfection. Standards of perfection stop us dead in our tracks because we know we will always be inadequate. Really good teachers have to be vulnerable, not perfect. I really like one of Parker Palmer's ideas—the one about teaching being this unique place where the public and private self intersects with an audience.[2] If you're constantly protecting yourself, you will never be a good teacher. And failing publicly in front of children who are like god-damned piranhas is a very frightening thing to do.

"I'm not saying that you need to be stupid. You're an adult, and they're children. You need to know what your boundaries are, where that line is. But if you never let them into your life, why the hell should they let you into theirs? Teaching is a human endeavor and is about people connecting with each other. If you're not vulnerable, you won't connect, and if you don't connect, you can't teach. That seems to me an elemental equation. If you want to maintain a barrier, teach in a university. Have that intellectual rigor that some people are so fond of. But I don't think you can teach children or make a difference in their lives if they don't trust you. When meeting somebody new, I don't think children, or anybody for that matter, really start to like someone until we see that person suck at something. How can you like somebody who's perfect? You can admire and respect them, but you can't like them.

"So I talk to my children about failure all the time. I show them failure. Just the other day, my co-teacher threw a bouncy rubber ball to me. I was supposed to catch it but am terrified of things being thrown at me. Not only did I not catch the ball, but I also batted it away and, in the process, caused it to bounce off a light fixture and right back into my head. I say to my students, 'Trust me about language, 'cause I'm really good at it. Trust me about all the stuff that I'm hired to teach you. But understand that I suck at a lot of stuff, too. Like, here's an example. Did anybody else nearly knock themselves stupid with a ball?' I think that is really critical to the process of connecting—to see people bomb out and do it graciously.

"I also say to my students, 'You guys didn't do a good job on this lesson because I didn't do a good job of telling you what you needed to know.' Do you know what a gift that is to give a twelve-year-old? To take the burden of failure off them and shoulder it yourself? And I have not yet burst into flames. I made a stupid mistake in front of a room full of children, but we're here to try another day. I talk to my student teachers about failure all the time because they don't need my help with success. Success is actually a naturally occurring phenomenon. If something's going well, you know it and roll with it. You need preparation for failure, not success, because obviously, another inspirational poster, if you're not failing, you're never going to get to that point that you want to be. We start at the wrong end with our student teachers, kids, and ourselves. We give lip service to 'you need to learn from your mistakes,' but everything we do belies our belief in that saying. I might add, 'you learn from your own failures, not anybody else's.' What you learn from someone else's failure is, thank God that wasn't me.

"I intentionally use the term *failure* rather than *experience. Experience* is a value-neutral term, and there's nothing value-neutral about failing. No matter what we call it, we all know when we bomb. When the kids have a really crappy lesson, and it's poorly thought out, and the goals are not clear, they struggle. They know that you're mad, and they're mad, too, because guess what? They don't want to fail either. So they're blaming you, you're blaming them, and we're calling this an experience? This isn't an experience; this is a disaster, and somebody needs to own that. One of the things I get better at the longer I teach is not only owning that failure but also helping the kids understand which part of it belongs to me and which part of it belongs to them. If I can't explain to them and myself what went wrong, I can't fix it. This is what's going on inside of me when I publicly call out my students on their failures. I name it and say who owns it.

"These are the kind of skills that make me a successful teacher to whatever extent that I am one. It's not learning more about the reading and writing part. That's important, and I do learn more about the content and hone my craft and lessons. But owning my failures so that I can legitimately ask the students to own theirs? I could not have done that six or seven years ago. I wouldn't have known how to do that. I would have been mad after a crappy class and said to myself, 'You guys are jerks. I'm up here trying to do my job, and am I getting any satisfaction from helping anybody? No,' because of, you name it: 'You're not raised right. You don't have any home training.' You know how that rap goes.

"I don't ever buy that the failure of children to fly and to be educated relies on money, computers, or books. If you've got nothing, then there you go. That's your lesson. 'We've got a problem to solve here, and we're gonna figure out as a community how to solve this. The fact that I'm your teacher only means that I have more experience in the world than you and can therefore guide and help you.' Please tell me this is not a *Reader's Digest* moment."

2

Developing Functional Literacy
for Social Justice?

As our five-person study group got to know each other over the course
of several months, significant individual differences emerged in philosophies and styles of teaching. Nevertheless, all of the teachers grappled
with a similar issue: Should they focus their time and energy on helping
students function in the current system or work to transform it? All of the
teachers in the study were subjected to the "conventional wisdom" (Tye
2000) that U.S. schools, like factories, should manufacture efficient workers and personally responsible citizens who can sustain the economy and
nation-state. As such, our monthly study group conversations regularly
focused on how the structures of schooling and our political economy
shaped their daily classroom interactions with students, colleagues, and
administrators. More specifically, we examined the forces promoting
education for obedient and disciplined workers, clients, and consumers
as well as the obstacles to cultivating skeptical, politically engaged citizens
committed to principles of equality and justice.

Eric Gutstein's (2006) book on teaching middle school mathematics
for social justice helped me identify in these conversations the teachers'
conflicted desire to develop their students' functional *and* critical literacies. Gutstein defines functional literacy as "the various competencies
needed to function appropriately within a given society" (5). Such literacy
"serves the reproductive purposes (i.e., maintaining the status quo) of the
dominant interests in society," which, in the United States, "are the needs
of capital" (5). Although proponents of functional literacy might make
the social justice claim that its cultivation enables students to participate

28

with other citizens in the U.S. polity and economy on relatively equal terms, a unique emphasis on the development of functional literacy in classrooms helps to create workers and citizens who sustain rather than challenge the current social order.

Moreover, a commitment to equal educational access through the universal development of functional literacy does not necessarily result in equal academic outcomes, particularly in our advanced capitalistic society. Depending on where our social order needs laborers to ensure a growing economy, functional literacy can thus include a curricular focus on basic computational, reading, and writing skills (the competencies needed for low-paid service jobs like burger flipping) or the ability to communicate, reason, and solve novel, ill-formed problems (the competencies required for white-collar "knowledge workers" like neurosurgeons) (Gutstein 2006).

In contrast to functional literacy, critical literacy enables students to "approach knowledge critically and skeptically, see relationships between ideas, look for underlying explanations for phenomena, and question whose interests are served and who benefits" (Gutstein 2006, 5). Critically literate individuals also know how to "examine one's own and others' lives in relationship to sociopolitical and cultural-historical contexts" and, importantly, can "recognize oppressive aspects of society so they can participate in creating a more just world" (Gutstein 2006, 6). Gutstein argues that the development of functional *and* critical literacies is necessary if we want U.S. schools to socialize students into questioning roles wherein they believe they have the power to shape the world (2006, 88).

In the rest of this chapter, I will highlight the advantages and limitations of emphasizing functional literacy in education for social justice. Because Margaret's teaching provides a particularly provocative, complex, and dynamic window into the significance of functional literacy for her students, the following pages highlight her perspective and practice.

A Powerful Lesson on Summarization

One month into the 2006–2007 school year, Margaret realized that most of her seventh graders did not know how to summarize information, something that the state's English language arts "model academic standards" required by the end of fourth grade. In the language of the state writing standards, incoming fifth-grade students should be able to produce pieces "that demonstrate the capacity to generate, focus, and organize ideas." Margaret thus put on hold her original curriculum, which included discussing and writing about how the power relations described in the novel *Touching Spirit Bear* (Mikaelsen 2001) related to those in her classroom.[1] In its place, she and her co-teacher, Vivian, taught a series of lessons aimed at helping students develop the summarization skills they would need for secondary education and beyond.

This work aligned well with Gutstein's (2006) definition of functional literacy: Margaret was teaching students a competency required for traditional academic success. Nevertheless, Margaret did not teach her students an elementary version of summarization. Rather, she situated the process of extracting and organizing information in the larger picture of knowledge construction. More specifically, she emphasized to the students that the content of their sentences for a summary paragraph of a text should be neither too specific nor too generalized by drawing a series of boxes that showed a spectrum of generality, ranging from generalizations to details (see figure 2.1).

As Margaret explained, she did not want her students to walk away from this activity thinking they had completed one more graded assignment that could be thrown away and forgotten. Rather, she wanted them to understand what they were doing when they summarized information so that they could enter subsequent classes or situations and effectively sort and sift information. Margaret, then, was helping students develop an understanding of the way written knowledge is organized, an important conceptual tool for doing far more than summarizing a single, short article. Her instruction brought to mind Lee Shulman's (1986) "pedagogical content knowledge," or the idea that talented teachers have distinctive forms of professional knowledge that guide effective teaching of their particular subject area with particular groups of students. In other words,

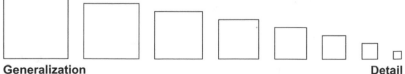

Generalization   **Detail**

Figure 2.1 Graphic of Knowledge Organization

Margaret knew how to integrate instructional principles and practices specific to language arts with language-arts-based content in ways that appropriately pushed her students' academic learning. This summarization lesson represented one of many instances that I observed Margaret identify difficulties her students were having in language arts and then adjust her pedagogy to meet their learning needs. In short, her skills-based teaching was aimed at developing a high level of functional literacy.

Nevertheless, Margaret's ability to teach functional literacy is only part of the story. Margaret expressed strong negative feelings about addressing systemic oppression with her students, which were articulated most clearly in the context of our monthly study group meetings. The following compiled dialogue from those meetings reveals Margaret's conscious rationale for focusing her instruction on the skills her students need to succeed in U.S. society as it currently exists and avoiding "the systemic search for the root causes of injustice" (Gutstein 2006, 7). After presenting the dialogue, I draw on my one-on-one conversations with Margaret as well as my observations of her classroom to critically examine the relationship between functional literacy and social justice.

Teaching Students to "Take Advantage" of the System?

MARGARET: It is interesting that in my context "taking advantage" seems like a good thing. I am desperately trying to teach my kids how the system works so they *can* take advantage of it.

CONNIE: But most of your students have been systematically disadvantaged.

JULIA: It does seem opportunistic and a little parasitic to "take advantage" if you start from a privileged place.

CONNIE: I was really struck by an argument that one of my professors, a linguist, made. He said that the main skill well-educated people learn is to talk expertly about their talents. For example, my sister's law firm asked her to write a self-evaluation when she was seeking a promotion. This exercise measured how well she could write about what she does, but a videotape of her interacting with her clients might have showed a discrepancy between her words and actions. I think this issue of spin mastery is one way that education can help already advantaged students take further advantage of the system.

JULIA: Margaret's kids are in a system where the people who run it and have power are often not the people they go home to. Because education is such a white, middle-class thing, academic success is not intuitive to many of Margaret's kids—they may not immediately understand what she is saying or what she wants them to do. In my school, I am dealing more with class than race or language issues, but I see middle-class kids being the most comfortable taking risks because school looks like home.

PAUL: My kids are definitely not struggling for survival. The expectation for most of my kids is that they will go on to college and become professionals in the future. Recently, I was listening to Ruby Payne talk about how to reach students from poor economic backgrounds, and she said that kids trying to survive often do not have long-term planning skills because they do not have the privilege of thinking about the future.[2] They have not practiced making choices for the future because they have to make decisions very quickly and move on to the next thing.

MARGARET: Poverty does require a much more in-the-moment way of living. It is all about what is going to happen to you tonight, not what is going to happen to you in ten years. I do worry that when people see my teaching, they think I am being patronizing to my students. I realize how differently I talk to these kids than I would to middle- and upper-middle-class kids. So when we start talking about social justice, I do not know if what I am doing is socially just or even involves a bigger framework. Sometimes I am just doing what will get me through my day. How is what I am doing going to help these kids be more successful in life ten years from now?

PAUL: Well, you are teaching them the skills to be successful in the dominant culture, if they choose to do that. It is asking a lot of classroom teachers in your situation to improve your students' future lives. I mean if society would change radically, that would help.

MARGARET: But is my school doing social tracking? There are few middle- and upper-middle-class role models for my children, which, in some ways, is preferable because those kinds of role models can diminish and marginalize students in a way that does not occur in my school. But is it social justice to isolate these kids during their middle school years in the name of offering them a safe emotional and intellectual space? I mean, even though our staff is really white, people in positions of power are African-American, and there are successful African-American parents who send there kids here instead of elsewhere because they want their kids in a place where they are in the majority during those really formative developmental years. But my kids' academic skills are so low, it makes me want to sit down and cry. When I asked my students to summarize a short article written at about a fifth-grade level, I discovered that they cannot write summaries. My analysis of their writing is that they do not know the difference between details and generalizations or how to use them in writing. So we have been isolating details—putting them into categories like "who" and "where"—and practicing making generalizations from those groups of details.

JULIA: Summarization is an example of a skill that comes up over and over again but often is not explicitly taught to the kids. I think teaching the students the lesson you just described will continue to help them after they leave your classroom.

MARGARET: As tedious as this process sounds, the kids were really engaged in it. They were not bored, which is my cue that they did not know how to do this. They wanted to learn how to do it, and I was pitching it at about the right level. The problem is going to come, of course, when I take away the life support. I don't know yet how I am going to wean them off the scaffolding.

PAUL: Are there English language learners in the class? Could language be part of the reason they don't understand the notion of a summary or the skills required to write one?

MARGARET: There are no students in the class whose Spanish is better than their English, spoken or written. This is not a second language issue; it is a cognitive issue.

PAUL: Well what is your theory about why they are struggling with summarization?

MARGARET: Given the context of American society and our educational system and, more specifically, the racial and economic makeup of my school, these kids are the least likely to know how to do this skill. Instead of having two of twenty-five kids in a class who do not understand a lesson, those two kids make up my entire class. They are all together in one spot.

PAUL: It just happened that way, or is it some phenomenon?

MARGARET: No, it did not just happen that way. We have developed a reputation in the district for being good with kids who have special education needs. I think in other local middle schools, a lot of the kids in our regular education program would immediately be identified and slotted for special ed. But more than that, I think summarization was never clearly explained to my students. It is astonishing how often I hear teachers say, "Well, I asked them to do blahdee blah, and they couldn't do it." I think in a lot of classrooms it stops at, "They should know how to do this by seventh grade," as if the teacher's job is simply to verify the fact that students lack this knowledge and give them an *F*.

PAUL: It's like a batch of product that comes down the line and is missing a part. Oh, well!

JULIA: Just last week, one of my middle-school colleagues said, "I don't know what teachers are doing at the elementary school, but students should be able to do this or that by the time they get to us." But when I was at the high school, I heard those same conversations about middle-school teachers. We just are not ready to accept students however they come to us.

MARGARET: Well, I have worked with a lot of people who cannot analyze kids' work down to the level I did in the summary lesson. We do not do enough mentoring and nurturing of young teachers. Maybe people think they are signing up for only sexy, fun stuff when they decide to become teachers. This summarization stuff is not that interesting to most teachers, and they think the kids are going to be bored. One recently certified colleague blatantly told me that grammar is not important to her teaching of Spanish. However, I know the population of students she is teaching. Their written and spoken literacy skills are all over the board. Some kids are from South America, others are from Mexico, and some kids were born in the barrios of East L.A.; yet she thinks that the structure of language is unimportant. She talks to the kids about political issues like immigration laws and gets them all excited about Americans not appreciating their stories. Of course the students are interested in these issues; they are intelligent children with lots of ideas. But way too many of them, more than sixty percent of them, do not have a really solid grasp of how to write a paragraph that makes sense. No matter what my students are good at and how smart they are, they will simply be buried if they go into high school with the academic skills they have now.

PAUL: In my classroom, we are fortunate to have two or three adults who can work with kids individually when we see they are struggling with a specific skill. We help the kids develop the skills they need to have, but, like this young teacher in your school, we also try to imbue a lot of the content we present with a political edge. We need to politicize kids to change society, which reminds me of Freire.[3] He said you cannot just parent students but also need to teach them discrete skills about how to deal with language. They need to know how to read the word *and* the world to be effective and have choices.

MARGARET: I do worry that I am too focused on skills. I also waste so much time dealing with kids' behavior that their thinking process is constantly interrupted during lessons. I am not delivering them any content, really, and I do not know what to do about that.

CONNIE: But I have seen you create lessons that help your students understand abstract concepts like power or fairness so that they can apply these ideas to situations beyond the classroom.

MARGARET: I guess I feel like I am reasonably successful at talking to kids about issues like power and justice because I keep the conversation very personal. I think that you head off despair by making children feel powerful; the weight of the world on a twelve-year-old or even a sixteen-year-old does not make anyone feel powerful. It is too much for them. It is too much for me. I cannot undo the world that they are living in, so I focus on helping them make the connection between achieving success in high school and the messages they send to other students and staff members through their behavior.

I am really blunt with the kids about the skills they need to avoid the loser classes in high school that channel kids absolutely no place except the unemployment line or prison. The classes where sixteen-year-olds get a workbook to fill in every day, and the teachers do not expect much from them. They know people who have been in those classes; many probably have brothers or sisters who have gone that route and dropped out. Academic failure is not a mystery to these children. The one thing that I do not talk to my kids about is the strikes against them because of their race. But I think they know it, and I know it. I do not come right out and say it because I do not think I can handle that piece of the discussion, given who I am. Somebody else is picking up that piece, and what can I do? There are racist people all over the world. If somebody is going to think that a kid is stupid because he or she is black, what can I do about that? Nothing.

I worry that discussions about racism and poverty allow my students to feel victimized and wallow in their powerlessness. They go out into the world not feeling like they can do things, and they are angry because if they are victims, then somebody has to be the oppressor. Whether the oppressor is white men, the military, the government, or whomever they want to demonize, they simply go out into the world as victims of that power structure and do not see their own efficacy. They do not see that there are ways that people can manage their power. Even if you cannot change the U.S. government, you can find places in this world to effect change. You know, my classroom is a place where I feel powerful and can do things that I think are good. But when I think too much about American public education, I want to go lock myself in a closet and drink. I always feel better, though, when I am in my classroom with my kids because I know what the boundaries are, and I know what I can do.

JULIA: I think there is an interesting parallel that just happened here. We are talking about what we can provide for our students and the awareness we can raise about the world and structures they live in. But we are on a parallel track as educators. In our school districts and with our coworkers, we are also trapped in a power structure. Since this is the system we have, and we are part of it, we need to figure out where our power lies so that we can get through the day-to-day stuff and try to make a difference.

Cultivating Functional Literacy
to Empower Individual Students?

During several group and one-on-one interactions, Margaret adhered to a belief in incremental rather than radical social transformation. In some respects, her commitment to empowering individual students to change the system aligns well with critical race theorists' emphasis on "the role incremental change can play in catalyzing more revolutionary change" (Tate 1997, 209). In other ways, however, Margaret and Paul's previous conversation about the cognitive differences between students from disparate socioeconomic backgrounds supported what Paul Gorski (2007) calls the "Ruby Payne Syndrome."

At an academic conference I recently attended, Gorski argued that Ruby Payne uses a cultural deficit model in her popular work on understanding economically poor students rather than a critical standpoint that addresses underlying class inequities. However, as activist, educator, and scholar Bill Ayers commented from the audience, Payne (2001) provides some tried-and-true strategies for teaching economically poor students in *A Framework for Understanding Poverty*. He further contended that a more powerful approach to challenging Payne's work than a podium-based, academic deconstruction of it would be to bring her book to economically impoverished communities and ask residents to speak back to it. Moreover, Julia, who attended the conference with me, pointed out that Payne's work is significantly more accessible to teachers than much of the esoteric jargon coming from the university. In the remaining pages of this chapter, I draw on Margaret's teaching to explore these competing arguments about effective educational approaches for equity and justice and to problematize theoretical warrants that ignore the contexts in which they are supposed to be implemented.

Asking Students to Assimilate in the Name
of Individual Empowerment?

I deeply admired Margaret's teaching talent but, toward the end of my yearlong study, became increasingly conflicted about her intentional evasion of acknowledging the systemic oppression that most of her students faced in their daily lives. After our eighth study group meeting, when she commented that she could not handle addressing racism with her students and did not think it served a valuable purpose, I asked Margaret if we could meet so that I could better understand her rationale for circumventing classroom discussions of macro-level, institutionalized social injustices.

Margaret was very deliberate about what she did and did not address in the classroom. I therefore suspected that I was misunderstanding an important piece of her instructional philosophy and hoped she would clarify her reasons for not integrating the issue of racism into the official curriculum. Before we met, I presented her with Gutstein's (2006) descriptions of functional and critical literacy and a short commentary by Janet McDaniel and others that claimed young adolescents are "developmentally capable of engaging in complex issues associated with social justice" (2001, 29). McDaniel and her colleagues conclude that middle-school teachers should help students become "the persons they want to become while also being explicitly and robustly anti-racist" (32).

Our one-on-one discussion, which took place in early November, included the repetition of claims that Margaret made during our study group conversations: She felt her students were not ready or able to look at issues of fairness and equity from a more global view but could develop an understanding of how these concepts related to their personal lives and relationships; she feared disempowering her students, promoting their victimization, and demonizing white people by addressing institutionalized racism. Margaret also emphasized the importance of teaching her students *how* to think, not *what* to think. Going into this discussion, I knew that Margaret resented the race-based assumptions that administrators, colleagues, and community members made about her. I also knew she did not want to "teach beyond herself" and felt like she did not and could not profoundly understand most of her students' experiences as working-class people of color living in a wealthy, racist country. Accordingly, it made sense that she did not want to teach lessons that risked perpetuating the notion that outward appearance alone captured a person's character and/or proffered the moral inferiority of some groups.

In several respects, I agreed with Margaret. Indeed, I continue to cling to an African-American female classmate's question in a graduate-level critical theory course that often felt disempowering. In effect, she asked the professor about the possibility of creating a third way rather than a reactionary "counter hegemony" that would replicate oppressive aspects of our current social order. Margaret was, in some ways, making

an argument that this student and feminist scholars like Elizabeth
Ellsworth (1989) have made. Ellsworth rocked the critical pedagogues
when she wrote,

> To the extent that our efforts to put discourses of critical pedagogy into
> practice led us to reproduce relations of domination in our classroom,
> these discourses . . . had themselves become vehicles of repression. To the
> extent that we disengaged ourselves from those aspects and moved in
> another direction, we "worked through" and out of the literature's highly
> abstract language ("myths") of who we "should" be and what "should"
> be happening in our classroom, and into classroom practices that were
> context specific and seemed to be much more responsive to our own un-
> derstandings of our social identities and situations. (1989, 298–299)

Margaret, like Ellsworth, felt trapped by the discourses surrounding
critical literacy. In her particular school, she saw two choices for her
teaching: to embrace the theory that "white people suck" and repeatedly
apologize for being white, or continue trying to help her students develop
personal efficacy in our racist world by becoming more aware of, and
therefore able to alter, their behavior in contextually appropriate ways.
Following our November discussion, however, I continued to disagree
with Margaret's claim that as a white woman she could not understand the
experiences of her students. Although I appreciated her refusal to embrace
the illusion of empathy—that she could understand in some complete
and total way the position of her students and their families—which she
felt often resulted in more pity than compassion, I also saw her negotiate
a third way with many of her native Spanish-speaking students.

One of the first things I learned about Margaret was her utter dedication to learning Spanish. She had begun to spend a month each summer
in a Spanish immersion program in Guatemala and paid an instructor
for formal Spanish lessons throughout the school year. She also received informal instruction from her native Spanish-speaking students
during class time and planning periods. Margaret's interactions with
these students seemed significantly less conflict-ridden than those with
her African-American students. Her overt valuing of Spanish in class,
particularly her continued insistence that every student in the class
should try to become bilingual, as well as her willingness to approach
the Spanish-speaking students as humble, unfinished learners, seemed
to create a bond with them that did not exist with many of her African-
American students.

To be sure, Margaret, much to the amusement of all her students, would integrate some student language into her teaching, such as "bogus" and "tweakin'," as well as make fun of her lack of knowledge of their world. However, she did not seem to embrace the cultural mores that accompanied some African-American students' language in the same way that she embraced those that accompanied Spanish, and her astute students picked up on this. When Margaret spoke Spanish to individual African-American students, for example, they frequently refused to try to understand what she was saying or would exclaim, "Speak English!" Additionally, Margaret told me that some students had accused her of favoring Latino students.

Despite the challenges she encountered in her relationships with some African-American students, Margaret both understood the cultural boundaries separating her from her students and designed instruction that built on students' prior knowledge while "stretching them beyond the familiar," two tenets of Ana Villegas and Tamara Lucas's "culturally responsive teach[ing]" (1998, xiv). Margaret also desperately wanted to prepare her students for future teachers and employers who would not see their cultural differences as resources but, rather, as "problems to be solved" (Villegas and Lucas 1998, xiv). This desire motivated her to teach the lesson, mentioned in the foregoing group dialogue, about avoiding "loser" high school classes and the academic failure that accompanied them. It was this lesson that pushed Margaret and my conversation about functional literacy in a new direction.

In part, the lesson on dead-end high school classes accomplished the teaching of "other people's children" that Lisa Delpit (1995) advocates. Margaret was trying to make explicit to her students the rules of the dominant culture's game, from which many were marginalized. However, she did not agree with Delpit's claim that teachers need to "acknowledge the inequity of the system" through open discussions of oppression before saying, "Let me show you how to cheat!" (1995, 165). Accordingly, Margaret and her co-teacher focused on the behavioral expectations of the "good" student who was both smart and able to negotiate the school system. They also contrasted this successful student with "Ollie," a fictional high school junior who had failed geometry, yelled at teachers when he became frustrated, and was suspended for starting a fight at school. After watching Margaret's co-teacher, Vivian, teach a lesson on Ollie's academic demise in early December 2006, I began to wonder what messages the students were hearing in these lessons on gaming the system. I worried that they felt they were being asked to become monocultural—to engage in the "subtractive schooling" that Angela Valenzuela (1999) so compellingly describes—rather than learn how to code switch in ways that did not undermine their positive identification with an African-American, Puerto Rican, Hmong, and/or other ethnic communities and heritages that were not Euro-American/white.

More specifically, during this lesson Vivian asked the students to offer some advice to Ollie that would improve his life and performance at school. I took particular note of an African-American female student's question and Vivian's response to it. The student asked if Ollie was perhaps not understanding what the teacher wanted from him and, as a consequence, failing academically. Vivian responded by saying that Ollie had failed his classes for two straight years of high school. If his failure was the teacher's fault, she went on to say, it was the fault of numerous teachers since Ollie had not done well in any of his freshmen or sophomore classes. Therefore, Ollie needed to take responsibility for his academic failure and not just blame it on his high school teachers. I wrote "Yikes!" in my field notes when describing this incident, as there was no recognition in Vivian's response of the systemic discrimination that many Johnson students face. I also wondered how the conversation would have changed if Vivian had responded to the student by asking, "What do you think is getting in the way of Ollie's ability to understand his teachers' expectations?"

I distinguished Vivian's response, based on the meritocratic ideal of personal responsibility (Westheimer and Kahne 2002), from Nancy Lopez's (2003) depiction of institutionalized racism against Dominican, West Indian, and Haitian-American youth in New York City. Lopez particularly noted the segregation of and harsh security measures against special education students, who were disproportionately male students of color, as well as the tracking of female students of color into low-level curricula, such as pink-collar secretarial training programs, that ultimately "undermined their prospects for social mobility" (2003, 168). Although we were far from New York City, there were plenty of black, immigrant, and refugee youth in Margaret and Vivian's classroom who would face institutionalized racism, albeit qualitatively different manifestations of it, in whatever high school they attended.

Consequently, I began to wonder if the intended lesson of helping students negotiate the U.S. educational system actually promoted the very despair that Margaret feared, as the students seemed to face a severe win-lose or lose-lose situation: work within the educational system as is and suppress an integral part of their identities or opt out of the system and, most likely, face detrimental, long-term consequences. Remembering my classmate's question in the critical theory course, I also wondered, was there not a third, fourth, or fifth way for Margaret's students? Did they have no possibility of successfully confronting and resisting an unjust teacher or educational policy? Could they not organize a critical mass of students to protest and demand change and/or seek out the backing of powerful stakeholders to assist them in their fight against injustice?

After class, I shared my concern with Margaret about the potential harm of the lesson's implicit message, and we once again scheduled a time to discuss this issue beyond school walls. I want to emphasize here that the mutual trust we had developed over a year's time made this exchange of vulnerabilities possible. It is also important to note that Margaret came to the table that night frustrated with aspects of the educational system that felt oppressive to her. A university consultant had recently come to her school and asked teachers to "rubber stamp" a curriculum she and other university-based educators had created, a process that invalidated Margaret's expertise as a seasoned curriculum developer. Moreover, when I mentioned particular student comments or behaviors in her classroom that suggested cultural misunderstandings, Margaret rightfully informed me of personal events in students' lives that made my generalizations about systemic oppression seem simplistic. I agreed with her that most people at the university have a long way to go when it comes to recognizing and valuing teacher knowledge and explicitly acknowledged the limitations of my understanding, as an outside observer, of her students' complicated lives.

As we continued to talk that December evening, an interesting shift happened, in part because Margaret linked her experience as a teacher in the hierarchical educational system and social order to that of her students, a connection she had made throughout the research process. We were discussing how Margaret, as a representative of the white power structure but also as an educator who had by and large earned her students' trust and respect, could make a powerful, positive impact on her students' lives, when I asked if openly acknowledging the "magnitude of the problem that people of color face in this country" (her words) might validate rather than victimize her students precisely because they believed she had their best interests at heart. I also speculated that Margaret's students might be relieved to hear from her that they were not imagining the ways in which our supposedly free and fair society was actually neither.

She associated the latter point with her own sense of powerlessness as a teacher and her resentment at being told time and again to be quiet and not create any waves. Margaret then wondered aloud if she was undermining her student's sense of cultural integrity by asking them to work within an educational system that often did not value or respect her or their communities' knowledge and customs. At our meeting's end, Margaret said she was seeing this "social justice business" in a new light and would think long and hard about additional ways to help her students succeed in the educational system without asking them to give up fundamental parts of themselves. I have no doubt that her commitment to teaching and, more importantly, teaching with intentionality, will enable her to tackle the similar yet different injustices of the educational system that she and her students face.

Conclusion

In this chapter, I drew on Margaret's teaching to argue that the development of functional literacy is crucial in K–12 education, especially for those students who do not enter the classroom already competent in the reading, writing, and numeracy knowledge and skills that are required to meet our society's current definition of academic achievement. As Margaret powerfully argued, political consciousness without the concomitant development of functional literacy can significantly undermine students' abilities to contribute to a more just world.

I also claimed that developing functional literacy is not sufficient for social justice education, as all students need to learn how to "recognize, understand, and critique current social inequities" (Ladson-Billings 1995, 476) if they are to participate in the co-construction of a more just society and world. In the next two chapters, I extend the arguments made thus far about functional and critical literacies to Joe's classroom, where the promotion of critical literacy abounded but so, too, did a problematic inattention to the development of functional literacy.

PART II

CRITICAL LITERACY

3

Critical Literacy in Context

A Portrait of Joe

I was sitting on Joe's deck, sipping a cup of his gourmet coffee and soaking up the warmth of a late spring morning, when a car pulled into the driveway. A sluggish teenager emerged from the vehicle and shuffled up to the table where I sat.

"Where's Joe?" he asked with a robot's monotone.

"He's inside calling other students about coming with us this morning. You're Tyler, right?"

He nodded.

"I recognize you from my visits to Joe's classroom. My name's Connie, and I'm a researcher at the university who has been working with Joe on a project. Since I can't go with you guys to North Dakota, I'm going to head out with you this morning to gather the willows that you're taking along."

Tyler asked, "Is there more coffee? Joe makes the best coffee."

"It's right inside," I responded. "Joe made a big pot."

In a few days, Tyler and five other students would drive to North Dakota and spend a month building structures for and participating in an annual Sun Dance ceremony. The students would receive physical education and elective credits for this work and, although Joe would not be compensated monetarily for mentoring the students, he felt that the valuable life lessons this experience reaped were reward enough. Plus, as he pointed out, he already planned to set the stage for the ceremony, so he might as well bring some extra hands.

I heard the screen door slam shut behind me as Tyler exited the house with a steaming mug in his hand. He sat down in one of the patio chairs across the table from me without making eye contact. Tentatively, I asked, "What year are you, Tyler?"

"A senior," he muttered.

"So did you just graduate?"

"No."

I looked down at my coffee cup, waiting to see if he would continue.

"I had kind of a rough night last night, so—"

"Fair enough," I interjected. "No more questions." I looked away from Tyler toward Joe's garden with its blushing strawberries.

We sat in silence for several minutes before Tyler began speaking again. "I was supposed to graduate this year, but ... " he paused, and I leaned forward to hear his quiet speech. "I was on academic probation this past semester and ended up failing some classes. But I just wrote a kick-ass letter to the teachers and principal about why they should let me stay for one more semester so that I can graduate. I'm expecting Joe to tell me what everyone thought of my letter today."

"I hope he has good news for you."

"I just need to try harder. I got a thirty-one out of thirty-six on my ACT but am failing out of school. What does that say about the way schools are run?"

"You make a good point, Tyler," I replied, wondering what process had transformed the hungover teenager of a few moments ago into this talkative education critic.

"I almost didn't get to go on this trip to North Dakota because I was arrested, and my court date was supposed to be in a couple of weeks."

"What did you get busted for?" I asked.

"Smoking pot." His face assumed an expression of annoyance.

"Well, I'm glad you can still go to North Dakota with Joe."

"Yeah, I'm looking forward to getting in shape. Man, I love this coffee."

"So you've been here, to Joe's house, before?" I asked.

"Yeah. I showed up fifteen minutes late for the ACT a couple of months ago, and they wouldn't let me take it. I knew my dad would yell at me, so I called Joe and came over here instead of going home. I sat out here and drank coffee with Joe and his wife, sister, and mom."

I was thinking about the many roles that Joe played in this student's life—stand-in father, friend, counselor, advocate—when he came out of the house carrying two sets of clippers. "It looks like we're the only ones who are going to be able to cut down willows this morning," Joe said with gentle resignation. "Connie, can you see if the chain saw is in the truck while I put these cups away?"

I nodded, and as I walked toward Joe's car, I heard him say to Tyler, "Everyone was impressed with your letter. I emphasized that you had been a strong contributing member to the school community for the past three years. You should be fine. Let's go."

After cutting, disbranching, and bunching willow stalks for the Sun Dance structures from a field beneath a Sam's Club parking lot, I learned why Tyler was still able to go to North Dakota. Joe and I had just dropped Tyler off when Joe told me he called the judge and explained to him that Tyler was supposed to be participating in a school-based service-learning project on his scheduled court date. The judge postponed the date without protest, and Tyler was able to accompany Joe to the Great Plains for a potentially life-changing experience.

Finding Joe

A local art teacher first told me about Joe. She worked at the private school where Paul, another teacher recruit, also worked, and I met her fortuitously on the way to a multicultural education conference. We exchanged contact information in the mayhem of airport shuttling and, happily, when I began recruiting research participants a year later, I found her e-mail address. She remembered who I was and responded immediately when I inquired, "Can you recommend any teachers of color in the public school system who might be interested in a collaborative study on teaching for social justice?"

"You should contact Joe," she wrote. "He teaches social studies and art, is Native American, and is a good friend of mine." Soon after, Joe invited me to his home to talk more about the project on a cold November evening.

As I parked the car on the street, I admired a cottage, which turned out to be Joe's sculpting studio, and expansive yard that accompanied the two-story light blue house. I walked up the long driveway in search of the main entrance and heard voices drifting in from the open garage. Inside, I found a man with longish black hair and a goatee, who appeared to be in his forties, a white, male teenager with dreadlocks, and two deer carcasses hanging from ceiling hooks. "Joe?" I asked tentatively as I reached the entryway of the garage.

"That's me. You must be Connie. I would shake your hand but mine are pretty filthy."

"No problem. Nice to meet you."

"This is my student, Steve," Joe said, pointing to the young man.

I nodded my head in Steve's direction.

"I hope the sight of dead animals doesn't gross you out." Joe continued to cut the fat from one of the deer while talking to me.

"No, not at all," I replied. "Actually, it brings me right back to my village in Africa. Eating meat usually went along with a visible sacrifice and gutting."

"Oh, yeah? Where were you in Africa?" Joe asked.

"Senegal. I was a Peace Corps volunteer."

"That must have been interesting. How long were you there?"

"Almost three years."

"I'm going to keep working, if you don't mind, while you tell me about this project of yours."

Joe and I proceeded to discuss my dissertation study as he apprenticed Steve in the art of dressing a deer. After a few minutes, Joe expressed interest in becoming a research participant. He also invited me to join him, Steve, and his wife for a venison steak dinner.

Life at Park High School

"There's a perception among lots of people that Park is a last-chance place," Joe said during our interview in his living room. "People think if a kid is not making it anywhere else, they can go to Park, take rudimentary courses, and get their diploma. But Park is not that. It's an alternative school for alternative's sake. It offers something else than what mainstream schools offer."

"When I was talking to an after-school program coordinator, she mentioned that Park is frequently associated with drugs," I said.

"That perception is still there, and it's not without merit," Joe confirmed. "But the fact of the matter is that the other high schools in town are also all about drugs. There's a huge drug culture in this city that every school has access to."

I nodded before saying, "One thing I wanted to make sure and ask you about is how you would characterize parental involvement at Park."

"It's a mixed bag," Joe responded. "Just like at any school, there are some parents who are very … active in the progress of their children's education. There are other parents who are very active in defending their children's behavior if they act up. We've had a number of them bring in the legal system to keep their kids from being kicked out. There are some parents who don't have the time or energy for school involvement. They are like, 'You have them six hours a day, you take care of it. I'll trust what you're gonna do.' I don't know if that's wrong. I know what it's like to be a blue-collar worker, because both of my parents were in that same boat. They didn't have the energy to deal with me or what I was doing in school. They just said, 'Well, if he's not truant, we'll let him do his thing,'" Joe said, laughing.

"And I failed out of everything. I didn't even get a diploma until I was much older. But I liked school. I liked learning in school. I just didn't like doing homework, so I didn't do the work, and I failed. My parents still didn't advocate for me. They didn't have time. Instead, they said, 'He'll make his way however he makes it.'"

"I remember you saying the dynamics are changing at Park. You specifically mentioned that test prep used to be more on the back burner at your school than it has been lately."

"There has been a lot of pressure coming from somewhere to up the ante with regard to *academic rigor*. Now, I don't really know what that term means. Does that mean more worksheets? We've always had kids write essays to gauge their academic progress. So if increasing academic rigor simply means more physical material to show what kids are learning, I have issues with that. I don't want to give kids 'make work.' I'd much rather gauge student learning through classroom discussions, and I'm not positive that our principal is comfortable with that. I think kids are developing intellectually in my classroom, but how do you measure that? That's the issue."

"In terms of the school's 'anti-ism' politics, do you think your principal's sexual identity influences how she directs the school?" I asked.

"We have five teachers in addition to the principal who are out, so Park is a safe place to be gay. The school allows you to be yourself."

"On a related note, could you talk a little bit about Park's antiharassment policy?"

"You can call people names all you want in the big schools," Joe replied. "There is no rule around that. That's First Amendment stuff. But that is no longer the harassment policy at Park. If students commit three verbal harassment offenses, they get kicked out. I do think, just because of the dynamics of our staff right now, the policy definitely emphasizes homophobia, not racism. Even when the students learn about the harassment policy during student orientation, the scenarios are about homophobia. I hadn't been paying much attention to this narrow focus until it was brought up recently. We're kind of pushing the envelope now to change that."

"I think you mentioned last time we spoke that you are one of two teachers of color at Park and that although your colleagues are somewhat like-minded, you're still dealing with issues, particularly around racism?"

"Yeah, race is more of an issue than anyone realized. It is so deeply institutionalized that if it doesn't get brought up once in a while, you don't even notice it. For example, one quarter we dropped nine black kids, and nobody saw anything unusual about that. Supposedly this high failure rate has nothing to do with the fact that these kids are black. They didn't know the school policy, or they didn't make probation. Therefore, they were out. It was very convenient.

"Finally, one of the math teachers, an old-timer, said, 'Do you see something wrong with this picture?' But still, nothing was changed. Nothing happened. I think our one African-American teacher, who is leaving Park at the end of this year, has been very forthright and adamant about making race an issue. When she is gone, I'm going to have to step into that role. Hopefully, her replacement will also be a racial minority. I don't know how many black teachers are available, though, to be honest. There aren't many in this district."

"There aren't many," I agreed. "There's a lot of irony in the fact that the school with the most antiracist mission in the district is demonstrating the same level of institutionalized racism as other schools. It's tricky because you see the effects of it, but untangling the process is much more—"

"Racism is deeply entrenched in every aspect of our society," Joe interjected. "Whether we want to recognize it and look at it or not, it's there."

Joe's Classroom

One look around Joe's classroom, located on the second story of the school building, indicated that craft making of various kinds took place there. Coiled baskets with handles, made from thin tree branches and thick rope, rested on shelves, and various electric tools and cords were stored along the walls. Joe's desk sat atop a long stage at the front of the room. The stage was made from wood covered with colorful writing, carved images, and drawings. During my first visit to Park, I learned that Joe made this stage from the students' former tables. Between fifteen and twenty students took an art class with Joe during the fall of 2005 to construct, decorate, and varnish new student tables, which filled the center of the spacious classroom and could seat up to six students each. Windows lined the wall across from the door. Peering out them, you could see the school garden, shaped like a sunburst, on the front lawn. Joe and his students had designed the garden and, during the fourth quarter, prepared and planted it for a class that included applying for U.S. Forest Service summer internships.

At Park, classes only lasted for one quarter, or nine weeks. Although the district and school administration expected Joe to go through the state social studies standards once a year and note which standards his classes addressed, Joe had a lot of leeway in what he taught and how he taught it. As Joe said during our interview, "Somebody determines what they think is important for kids to come away from high school learning, and, to some degree, I would agree. You know, some level of understanding of how the government works. But ... there's no real explicit rules on how you [do that, so] ... I choose to teach a class on civil liberties." As a social studies and art teacher at an alternative school, Joe was able to teach a wide variety of courses: environmental studies, state history, an "open mike" class wherein students sang, played instruments, and/or did spoken word, introductory anthropology, a class on Daniel Quinn's work, a wilderness experience class that included a trip to the Ozarks, Native American basket weaving, and African drum making, to name just a few.

The broad spectrum of subjects about which Joe could teach demonstrated his insatiable curiosity about the world and passion for learning how to do new things. The drum-making class, for example, required that Joe not only be apprenticed by a local African musician in the art of making *djembes* but also that he figure out a way to obtain the wood needed for twenty drums. As an accomplished wood sculptor, Joe knew how to wield a chain saw and so was able to master quickly how to shape the drum shells that his students would design, cover, and learn how to play during the course. While describing this class to me during our interview, Joe revealed his awareness of and attention to indigenous cultural practices. He had been concerned about the sacrilege of creating a drum for purely utilitarian reasons because, in his Native tradition, drums were spiritual, and people were allowed to make only four during a lifetime. Only after the Ghanaian musician assured him that he was not transgressing sacred cultural norms did Joe teach the class.

The hallway leading to Joe's classroom contained numerous photos of his outdoor adventures with students. With a zest for "experiential learning education," Joe had taken students on eight two- to three-week trips during his years at Park. The trips included a service-learning component, such as building trails, and, usually, some sort of camping experience. Joe loved getting to know his students and discussing the state of the world with them around a campfire, outside the structured setting of the classroom. As he said, "The experience of pushing at kids' limits and making them rely on each other for real things ... to get something done so that they can eat ... that's so much more valuable than anything you can do out of a book." Although some administrative glitches and a funeral prevented his wilderness experience class's spring trip from taking place, Joe intended to take interested students on an additional, non-school-sanctioned backpacking trip in the Ozarks during spring break.

Students either passed a class or did not at Park and, in Joe's social studies classes, passing usually required the writing of at least two essays as well as class participation. At the end of the quarter, students wrote individual course evaluations that allowed them to assess their "experience in the class and how they feel they did." These evaluations gave Joe helpful feedback on students' perceptions of the course. Subsequently, Joe wrote his evaluation of each student's performance. If students applied to college, the admissions office received these written evaluations rather than transcripts with a quantified GPA.

During social studies classes, Joe usually read aloud, or asked students to read silently, books like Paul Loeb's (2004) *The Impossible Will Take a Little While.* They would then discuss as a class the ideas and information presented in the texts. These discussions were informal, and Joe often told personal stories or jokes related to the book's themes. He was well known in the school for his jovial, sometimes vulgar sense of humor. While I observed Joe's classes, I learned that he had traveled to Europe for a wood carving competition, ruptured his eardrum in the military, and had all but an arranged marriage with his first wife, whom he met while in the service. These tales both endeared Joe's students to him and helped to keep them engaged in classroom conversations. A Public Broadcasting

Service (PBS) addict, Joe was also a fount of knowledge about numerous phenomena and historical events, such as the environmental effects of suburbanization and the French and Indian War. What follows is an example of a typical conversation in one of Joe's social studies classes, taken from my field notes:

Almost ten minutes after the class period has started on a cold January afternoon, students continue to trickle into Joe's wilderness experience class. Joe says, "Six of the eighteen students in this class were late today. This is bad, bad, bad. Let's not make a habit of this. All right, come up and get your copy of *Listening to the Land*.[1] This is one of three books that you will be reading and reporting on for this class, and we're going to start reading it today. I think you'll really like it."

Individual students come up to Joe's desk to sign out books. Joe speaks informally to them as they do so, asking one student how his training for the local marathon is coming along and another how he manages to keep his baggy pants on his hips without a belt.

After all of the students have a book, Joe directs, "Everybody listen up. Please open your books to Christopher Manes's interview about radical environmentalism on page fourteen. We are going to skip the first interview, because it is too over the top, even for me. Ross, if you don't mind stopping your personal conversation, I would like to start class."

Joe begins reading the introduction about Manes who is the author of *Green Rage,* but one of the female students continues to speak to a fellow student sitting beside her.[2] Joe looks up and says, "Jen, I was sharing deep insights here. Do you mind?"

Jen sighs, puts her feet, encased in combat boots, on the table, and opens her book. Joe continues to read about Manes's work to address the deleterious environmental effects of the postmodern era. The introduction says that part of Manes's documentary has been shown on MTV, inspiring Joe to say, "I guess the MTV audience is going to make the most sense of Manes's suggestions because their minds are as malleable as silly putty. Actually, I was part of the MTV generation."

"I've heard we're part of the bling-bling generation," a student dressed entirely in black retorts.

Ross adjusts his woven Rastafarian cap and declares, "Most people in this generation are a bunch of narcissistic fuck-heads who are apathetic and materialistic."

Another male student, who is playing with his tongue stud and wearing a black cape, chimes in, "Well, fifty years down the road, money won't

Critical Literacy in Context 53

buy anything because there will be nothing left to buy. Then, they'll
have to do something."

"Why is it always fifty years?" Ross snaps.

"Okay," Joe says, "let's say by 2007, Toyota makes all of its vehicles
hybrids, and they get two times the gas mileage of most cars currently
on the road. Would that be enough to save the planet?"

A male student brushes his blond dreadlocks away from his face before
saying, "The oil companies won't let that happen. Plus, hybrid cars don't
clean up polluted water or change the overpopulation problem."

"I'm inclined to agree with you, Sean," Joe replies. "We don't have
solutions to these problems yet."

"Toyota's only trying to increase its sales with the hybrids anyway,"
Ross adds. "It's all about capitalism and the bottom line."

"Ford did lay off thirty thousand of its workers yesterday," Joe replies.
"The company said it was making too many cars and so now is going to
focus on making better cars with a third of the workforce."

The student in black yells, "Snap!"

"People who were working there for twenty years are suddenly los-
ing their jobs," Joe continues. "It's pretty tragic." He then redirects his
attention to the book, reading aloud the first sentence of Manes's essay
before asking, "What do you think he's getting at?"

A female student who is wearing a fashionable sweater and has her
hair pulled tightly into a ponytail is the first to answer. "He's saying
that people are indifferent to the harm they're causing the environment
through their overconsumption of things."

"Yeah," Joe agrees. "We're seeing the world as a resource to be used
rather than something to nurture and sustain."

"It's not just indifference," Ross jumps in. "We're not connected to the
ecosystem anymore. We don't understand where our food comes from or
what the effects of constantly exploiting the earth's resources are."

"Wow, you got that from the first sentence, Ross?" Joe asks. "That's
pretty cool."

Joe's Path to Teaching at Park High School

"I was born and raised in rural Maine, the child of a French and Native
mill worker and his young Filipina wife, whom he met in Okinawa while
in the military. My mom came to America thinking what most people

think of America in the twentieth century and ended up in the back woods of Maine," Joe said, laughing. "We were the only brown people in our entire town.

"A number of things were part of our upbringing," Joe continued. "(A) Don't draw attention to yourself, you know, don't make trouble. Just be," Joe paused. "Just be a fly on the wall, and (B), if that fails, don't come home beat up. If you get beat up, you better fight back."

"So did you stay in Maine until ..."

"Just until I was old enough to get out" Joe laughed. "Then I joined the military for ten years."

"Wow," I replied, aware that I did not have an articulate response to his life account, which differed dramatically from my suburban childhood and subsequent college experience.

"I joined the service to get away, really just to get out of there, on the advice of my father. I would have been a fourth-generation worker in that paper mill, which is probably going to shut down in the near future. But my dad said, 'You need to get out of here and try something different,' which was insightful for a relatively uneducated guy who had lots of flaws. So that's what I did. I never intended to be a career man, but I stayed in the service because I liked to travel, and I traveled all over. It was really enjoyable because I happened to be in the military during ten years of peace. Then, do you remember when we bombed Libya?"

"Umm ... " I tried to remember the year of this bombing but only recalled that I was a child when it took place.

"We had been at this site doing maintenance," Joe continued. "We would be gone about ten months a year, all over NATO. I was in Europe at the time, and, to save money, my team had been camping rather than spending our per diem money on hotels. Anyway, we went to the site the day after we bombed Libya, and it was crawling with people in their war gear. They had gas masks on, and we had no idea what was going on. They made us put our IDs on the ground and put our hands behind our heads because nobody was supposed to be there.

"So we smelled of wood smoke," Joe laughed, "when we came upon not just enlisted people but also officers who gave me a lot of flak (since I was the chief of the team) about our scruffy appearance. At that point, I thought if we are going to be at war, I don't want to be doing this. So I decided I had to get out and go to college.

"I had had three new guys on the team who came straight from basic training, and we were teaching them on the job. I thought teaching them was pretty cool, so I decided to go to college and become a teacher. And that's what I did."

"Did you go to college out East?" I asked.

"I came here. I didn't even have a high school diploma at that time, so I called the university and started inquiring about what I needed to do to enroll. When the university received my high school transcripts—and I had the lowest GPA of my entire high school class of two hundred twenty-four kids—someone called me and said," Joe laughed, "'How can we let you in? You have to go to school for a year and prove that things have changed.' At that time, I had been reassigned to Mississippi and had one year of military service left. I was able to get a job in public affairs so that I could stay in Mississippi and go to night school at a nearby junior college. I got thirty credits over the course of that year and received straight *A*'s, so the university let me in. From the beginning, I wanted to be in the education department."

"Did you get your teaching certification in secondary social studies?"

"And anthropology," Joe replied. "I had enough anthropology courses for a double major and so got certified in that as well. I ended up student teaching where I teach now and just fell in love with it."

"I didn't know you student taught at Park."

"Yeah. I remember being in an educational foundations class, and one of the Park math teachers as well as three or four students came in as guest speakers. I was so impressed with the way these high school kids were talking and with what the teacher had to say. They emphasized that the cornerstone of the school was not ACT preparation but critical thinking, which is the foundation of the Park social studies department. We try to teach these kids how to be more than productive members of a consumer society. Park is also known as a safe school for kids who have been most marginalized by the system.

"After I graduated, I decided that Park was where I needed to teach," Joe continued. "So I approached the principal, who told me there were no openings in social studies. Most teachers don't leave the school until retirement, so I essentially went to graduate school in art to kill time. There were no GRE requirements," Joe laughed, "and it was a program that required the least amount of pain. I've always made baskets and stuff, so I just used the things that I had already made to create a portfolio, and they said, 'Come on, you're in.' I spent three years getting a master's of fine arts."

"Did you start teaching at Park right after graduate school?" I asked.

"No, I had to teach at one of the district's other high schools for three years to get my foot in the door since there were still no openings at Park. The principal at Park told me my best shot was to transfer in from another district school, so I went to Grover High School for an interview and," Joe snapped his fingers, "got the job. I knew I had the position right away because the principal was under a lot of pressure from the African-American community to (A) create an African-American history class as one of the required U.S. history classes, or at least as an option, and (B) not have a blonde, blue-eyed woman teaching the class.

"When I walked in as a minority man," Joe snapped his fingers again, "I could see it in the principal's eyes that I was hired. But when I got the job at Grover, there was a blonde, blue-eyed woman who had a master's degree in African-American history. She filed a grievance with the union because she was clearly more qualified than I was to teach a course on African-American history. Under the circumstances, they promised her the next available job, and she backed off.

"I got the job in mid-July and for the rest of the summer learned what I could about African-American history. I ended up teaching the course for one year because an African-American female teacher, the daughter of a local activist, was hired. Then I was moved into Latin-American history, which I also knew nothing about," Joe said, laughing. "That course was given to me the day before school started, and I just thought, oh man, what am I supposed to do?

"So while I was learning some Latin-American history, I taught a unit on physical anthropology, which I justified by saying, 'If we're gonna even study the people who first lived in South America, we need to talk about how they got there. And if you talk about that, you've got to talk about the evolutionary process.' So we went from Australopithecines to the peopling of South America over a five-week period. By then, I had some material and was able to dive into Latin-American history."

Joe's Instructional Approach

Joe's style of teaching led many students to talk to him like a friend or counselor. Consequently, several students often asked him for advice or favors, like giving them a ride home or cashing their paychecks.

When a Native student told Joe she was thinking of becoming pregnant, he responded in a kind but resolute tone, "Teenage pregnancy equals poverty." I recognized the extent to which Joe understood the realities of his students' lives while talking to him the day after a Park alumnus died of a suspected drug overdose. Joe related that after this student publicly insulted the principal at his graduation ceremony the year before, several teachers proposed his banishment from the Park community. In response, Joe sent an e-mail to staff members, emphasizing that this student had an obvious drug problem and that excluding him from a supportive social network could be harmful. "Do you really want to be called into the office next year and find out something terrible has happened to Peter?" Joe had written. Unfortunately, Joe's prescience did not prevent this exact scenario from taking place.

As my relationship with Joe developed, he revealed his growing unhappiness with working at Park and his mounting uncertainty about the legitimacy of his participation in my study. He was not feeling as connected to his students as he usually did and worried that I was wasting my time in his classroom. Joe did not think he qualified as a social justice educator. Moreover, his antiauthoritarian approach to teaching meant he frequently butted heads with the principal, whom Joe saw as too "rules-oriented." Increasingly, he clashed with other teachers as well. The staff was trying to implement a unified approach to school policies, such as attendance guidelines, and Joe often refused to enforce them. Accordingly, he felt that many teachers saw him as a troublemaker. Perhaps more detrimental to his intra-school relations, however, was Joe's refusal to wear a "teacher hat."

Joe's informality in a school that adhered strictly to its anti–verbal harassment policy was a recipe for trouble. Although most students seemed to enjoy Joe's "non-PC" jokes about, for example, race, gender, and sexuality, others did not, as was evidenced by Joe's admission that the principal had placed some official student complaints in his file. Moreover, although I heard Joe explicitly tell one group of students at the beginning of a quarter that he wanted them to feel comfortable in his room and that anytime he teased a student, it only meant Joe liked him or her, his laid-back teaching style did not necessarily suit students who wanted and needed the adults in their lives to set clearer boundaries. Consequently, the very behavior that enabled Joe to build strong relationships with several students also served to threaten his career at Park.

Joe recognized the need to be more vigilant about his offhand remarks to students, especially since he suspected that the principal was looking for a reason to push him out of the school. However, his belief in "just being Joe" seemed nonnegotiable. His rejection of a more distanced, professional identity in the classroom relates to Kenji Yoshino's (2006) argument, based on psychoanalyst D. W. Winnicott's work, about the "True Self" and the "False Self." According to Yoshino, "The True Self is the self that gives an individual the feeling of being real" and is "associated with human spontaneity and authenticity" (185). "The False Self, in contrast, gives an individual a sense of being unreal, a sense of futility" (185). Nonetheless, "The False Self has one positive and very important function: to hide the True Self, which it does by compliance with environmental demands" (185). In other words, the False Self is sometimes needed to protect the True Self in social situations and can thus be helpful so long as it has "as its main concern a search for conditions which will make it possible for the True Self to come into its own" (185). In sum, Yoshino argues that a minimum False Self, or level of assimilation, is necessary to "regulate relations between the True Self and the world" (86). Joe seemed to be fighting the expression of any False Self, even though *some* accommodation of school regulations and norms would better protect his job and, in turn, potentially make his relationships with his colleagues, boss, and some students less painful to navigate.

In August 2006, Joe found out that funding fell through for a project that would have allowed him and nine other Native American teachers to pursue a graduate degree in educational administration, a degree that would have opened the door to Joe's dream of starting an experiential school. He thus steeled himself for another year of working within the constraints of school walls.

Joe's Educational Philosophy

"You are really good at engaging students in conversation, which seems to be one of the most difficult things for teachers," I said. "I'm thinking specifically of how, according to this study I read, many teachers rely on the IRE model: A teacher *initiates* a question, a student *responds,* and the teacher *evaluates* the student response before moving on, to find the correct answer or ask a new question.[3] Anyway, everything is very teacher-driven in the IRE approach, and students do not engage in ongoing conversations. It can be terrifying to ask more open-ended questions, and many educators do not seem comfortable facilitating the more difficult process of unpredictable dialogue."

"Well, I don't see teaching as a profession," Joe replied. "I don't see teaching as a role because I'm not," he paused. "I'm not any different when I'm with a kid than I am with you right now. I don't know how to turn that off. I'm just me. But that translates very clearly to the kids. They may lack the articulateness to really explain it, but they'll say, 'You're really real, Joe. Geez, you're really real.'

"I've always seen that as a compliment," Joe continued. "I had never really thought about what that meant until I was told, 'For Christ's sakes, be a professional!' But teaching isn't a profession for me. It's just my, it's kind of my life. That's why I take kids to summer ceremonies in North Dakota, spend my spring break on backpacking trips with them, and have them come over to my house a lot. I do things with kids that go way beyond the contract, things that I think would be good for them. I don't know how to turn it off, and I wouldn't turn it off. In the traditional schools, it was a little easier to turn off because I had a stack of essays this big," Joe created an imaginary two-foot pile of papers with his hands, "to correct by Monday. I didn't have time to do a lot of things. It's different at Park. The classes are a lot smaller, no more than fifteen to twenty students, and I'm not doing four sections of the same course. Usually, I teach four different courses each semester.

"You know, kids don't always do great work, which might just reflect their lack of skills in writing or motivation. But if I'm giving essay questions that are not found in the book, students have to think—to correlate or compare something. If they're interested, kids respond well to those. Their grammar or writing might suck, but this is not what is important. It's important that I ask them a question just because I want to know what they think."

"So it seems like, in some ways, you're rejecting the model of professional expertise and that sort of technical, I-know-more-than-you knowledge that is associated with it," I said.

"Absolutely. Absolutely," Joe replied, nodding his head. "I just don't buy it. I'm sure there are a lot of social studies teachers, maybe the majority of them, who would completely disagree with me that content isn't important. I just don't think it's important because two weeks from now, you may have done well on the test, but you're not gonna remember any of the content. That was certainly the case in my college experience, and

I did well in college. I didn't learn a lot; I just learned how to study. I learned how to take a test and write a paper."

"So the skills that kids are lacking, like writing skills, do you see it as central to your job to develop those?" I asked, feeling somewhat conflicted about Joe's statements about academic content and skills.

"Oh, certainly to help," Joe replied. "Not to make them expert writers but to point out that their lack of skills is problematic and that they need to work on them. But kids are motivated to learn something that interests them or that they need. For example, if they need to know something to get a job, they're gonna learn it. But if they're in a class that doesn't interest them in any way, shape, or form, they're not gonna perform for you. They're not gonna care. Content comes with interest. If I plant a seed that they find interest in, that's great. I think the content in my classes is pretty interesting stuff, but it is far less important than the processes of thinking about and discussing the issues."

"While talking to you, I keep thinking about this sociological teacher profile that I read about for a class.[4] According to this scholar, the vast majority of teachers were successful students, which I think often creates conflicts in classroom settings because these teachers expect students to have their same cultural model—their same view of the world and schooling. And this model is often associated with a middle-class, white perspective."

"That's so interesting," Joe replied. "When I taught at Grover, before coming back to Park, about seven teachers made up an old white man's network in the social studies department. They were all closing in on retirement, and I could tell that they were looking at each other and thinking, 'Who is this weird guy? Is he going to create good, civic-minded individuals? I bet he doesn't. I bet he's one of those people who's gonna try to get the kids to think critically,'" Joe said, laughing.

"These history teachers saw their role as the creation of patriots," Joe continued, "and I just completely disagreed with it. I think our role is to give kids tools to think critically, to think for themselves. Let them make judgments that are based on a process rather than the word of the Heavenly Father. That's been my focus with the kids from day one, and I'm still learning how to teach them these tools. It's not an easy thing to do, but it's the right thing to do."

4

The Limits of Critical Literacy in Isolation

If humans can create a social system that always puts profit above human needs—capitalism—then human beings can develop alternatives that put people first.

—*Eric Gutstein,*
Reading and Writing the World with Mathematics

My son can tell you all the reasons why sweatshops are bad, but the last time he sent me an e-mail, I wanted to go out and buy him a dictionary.

—*Paraphrased statement by parent of Park alumnus*

Joe's portrait highlighted his use of critical pedagogy to promote a social system that puts both human and environmental needs above profit. It also exposed his disdain for rote forms of teaching and learning, particularly when they revolve around standardized testing.

The urban public school district in which Joe and Margaret worked was somewhat shielded from the neoliberal dictates of *No Child Left Behind* (Hursh 2006). Although we sensed that more rigorous impositions for standardized test preparation were impending, these public school teachers had a much greater sense of autonomy than has been reported in cities like Chicago (Lipman 2004) and Houston (McNeil 2000a, 2000b). Nevertheless, district budget cuts meant Joe had to spend more time fund-raising for the school activities that he valued, such as a weekly community lunch wherein the new students cooked a meal for the rest of the school. Money for books, class supplies, and professional development also dwindled as the district in which Joe and Margaret worked continued to lose money.

In the following pages, I examine the notion of critical literacy within this larger economic and social context where "the neoliberal managerial strategy 'disproportionately empowers residents who are already endowed with the forms of social and cultural capital necessary to navigate through bureaucratic systems while in effect ... punishing people who are least likely to have the social skills and resources necessary to obtain goods and services that they are most likely to need'" (Klinenberg, in Pattillo 2007, 151). More specifically, I focus on the tensions involved in teaching for critical literacy within a social institution—schooling—that has historically prioritized functional literacy and social control (Gutstein 2006). In this historical moment, Joe's teaching offers a particularly fraught example of using critical literacy to bring about positive social transformation. The parent's quote that opens this chapter strikes at the heart of the matter: How can the development of critical literacy advance both individual students' academic success—which is linked to social mobility opportunities—and systemic social change?

To begin responding to this question, I present a compiled dialogue from our study group meetings. This conversation reveals the dynamic relationship between the contextual specificities of each teacher's school and the macro-level economic, political, and social pressures that shaped the teachers' approaches to cultivating critical literacy in their individual classrooms. I then examine the advantages and limitations of Joe's approach to teaching critical literacy before addressing the problematic, widespread practice of hierarchically ordering oppressions in talk about educating for social justice.

Should We Endorse "Shutting All the Doors"?

JOE: I have a very hard time getting my students to think about anything besides their own little worlds. It is all about me, my hormones, and my music. I have found that the majority of my students want to play and be allowed to avoid any reading or writing. That is really unfortunate because these kids who do the minimum amount to pass will not be successful in college if that is where they want to go.

PAUL: My kids are self-absorbed and oblivious to things at times, too. But most of them bring a lot of cultural capital to the classroom. Many are well traveled, and their families share certain cultural markers, like reading the *New York Times* or listening to National Public Radio. Once their parents see that I do these things, too, I am accepted as part of their club, and they trust me. These shared activities and experiences often allow for more sophisticated classroom conversations about world events and social issues, which are not alien to my students. I like to think that I introduce them to new information and ideas, but I don't know.

MARGARET: The social justice issues I deal with are largely ones of race and class, and you don't get much bigger issues than that. I am constantly aware of the fact that I am white and, economically speaking, way better off than eighty-five to ninety percent of the students who show up in my classroom. It seems unlikely that I would still be teaching at Johnson if I had not been open to meeting my students where they were at. Ten years ago, I would have said my job was to be a good role model for the students and teach them about the world—my world, the adult world, whatever I would have labeled it. But sometimes I am stunned at how much the students have changed me. If you are going to have real social justice, there has to be some sort of exchange. In my position, I did not really choose to give up power. It was pretty much taken away from me, and we renegotiated what I could have and what did not belong to me anymore.

JOE: *Negotiation* is the key word, I think. Power was not taken away in a punitive sense. You negotiated and evolved. I think in most school settings, the pecking order of administration, teachers, and students makes the teaching of social justice difficult because the students experience a hierarchy of haves and have-nots at school. One of my highest priorities has been to establish a different kind of classroom in which schooling is not just about me having power over the students but, instead, creating relationships based on the sharing of information and my attempt to communicate the wisdom I have acquired from forty-eight years of living on this earth.

However, we are getting more of your clientele, Margaret, and classroom management has become necessary, which is new to me. Park is a very different place than it was three years ago, which is not all negative. We have lost fewer students to attendance issues because we have a lot more African-American kids who are not habitual skippers. A significant number of these kids come to school to be in school, though not necessarily to focus and learn. Now the challenge is to work on getting those students engaged in doing school.

PAUL: Well, our society does not promote student engagement by insistently judging students according to how well they fit into the capitalist system, or even into the higher educational system. There are all these external forces acting on students. The neoliberals and neoconservatives are trying to replace the public educational system with a privatized one—

JOE: A for-profit educational system.

PAUL: —where their children can go to whatever elite schools they want. I do not know the grand scheme, but it seems like *No Child Left Behind* is attempting to dismantle public education.

JOE: This desire not to publicly fund the educational system comes at a time when the student demographic is changing. We are now getting kids who are in such survival mode that to sit down and talk to them about subjects like philosophy is impossible. Brenda, one of Margaret's former students, is a prime example. I will not advocate for her to stay at Park when she flunks all of her classes for the second time this quarter because she has physically threatened me. What is worse, she is not alone. There are seven students currently in that zone.

MARGARET: I don't mean this as a criticism of Park, but I have sort of lost a sense of what your school's mission is, Joe. Now, a lot of kids say to me, 'Park is a place for losers.' I try to counter that view, but it seems like there is a certain kind of kid that makes it there and then a revolving undercurrent of kids for whom Park is one more thing on the list of stuff they tried and failed at. Is that at all accurate?

JOE: It is accurate. Part of the problem is funding cuts. You cannot sustain anything but preparing kids for "Leave No Child Untested" when you cut ten million dollars a year for five years in a row from the district's operating budget. Many of the alternative programs no longer receive funding, so more and more kids are being funneled toward Park. Rather than remaining an alternative school for alternative's sake, we are becoming the dumping ground for all of the at-risk kids. There is also staff resistance to remedying this revolving-door problem. We pay a lot of attention to teasing of the fat gay kid but no attention to the constant racial tensions. We recently had an antiracist hip-hop group perform at a school celebration. All of the white kids sat in the left bleachers, and all of the black kids sat in the right bleachers. It made me so sad.

PAUL: We live in a capitalist system where the white males who created the system largely continue to sustain it. How can we encourage people to get to the point where at least on paper, if not visibly, they are of equal status with white men and are therefore in a position to change the whole thing? And, since being successful within a system often corrupts visions of trying to change things, how can we help those who are committed to change get into positions of power?

JOE: Our capitalist system certainly would not function if every kid went to college. Capitalism really does not want no child left behind. It needs some left behind to be burger flippers and janitors. Hopefully, the kids who grow into adulthood doing these jobs will realize that seven-fifty an hour is not cutting it and think about returning to school. But all this talk about *No Child Left Behind* is just make-believe. If all kids were doctors, lawyers, and Indian chiefs, our system would not work. Public schooling was originally designed to keep kids out of the workforce so they would not take jobs away from needy adults. I suppose that college may be the best way to continue your education after high school in today's world, but why not let kids live and experience the world for a while if that is what they want to do?

MARGARET: I agree that kids need to hear they have options besides college. But if I say it as a white middle-class woman, many people think I do not believe in these kids. In a recent class, I asked how many students planned to go to college. Twenty-one little hands went up in the air. So I asked, "How many of you like school?" Every hand went down. Then I asked, "What do you all think you are going to be doing in college?" It was a rhetorical question, but this conversation revealed the disconnect between the ideal and reality of going to college. I do not think it is social justice to tell every child, regardless of his or her academic skills or feelings about school, that college is both possible and desirable—to set kids up with only one possible option for success. There are other jobs in the world besides neurosurgeons and burger flippers. A lot of people do not go to college, and a large percentage that start never finish. They all must be doing something. These kids' parents are not neurosurgeons or burger flippers, but my students do not see their home realities reflected in schools because we give them the choice of going to college or working at McDonald's.

PAUL: Well, if our government did a better job of taking care of every member of society, we might have a different view of education's purpose—something more like European folk schools, which emphasize enriching our culture rather than succeeding in the marketplace.

JOE: Or our military, which is also a major part of the marketplace.

PAUL: It is not easy to impact kids in ways that help them become conscientious members of society. Part of my teaching includes trying to live a quality life in the here-and-now with an eye toward the future, but not a total eye. It is a horrible existence to learn and do everything because you will need it in the future, for a standardized test. As a teacher, I want to encourage the kids to be the best that they can be but also separate happiness from success in the marketplace. I think it is really important for kids to question college as *the* measure of success in our culture.

JULIA: If you had to ballpark it, Paul, how many kids at your school go on to college?

PAUL: At least ninety percent.

JULIA: Listening to your definition of success, I am thinking about my own promotion of marketplace success. It seems like you have the luxury of asking if traditional success leads to happiness because so many of your students are already on the college track. I am afraid that if I deemphasize marketplace success, the students are going to think I am discouraging them from pursuing higher education. For a lot of kids, I find the most effective way to emphasize continuing their education is to say, "There is a comfortable lifestyle that you are going to want and, in this world, money opens a lot of avenues."

PAUL: Well, regardless of what I teach, many parents—even the professed liberals and progressive thinkers—become neoconservatives and neoliberals when it comes to their own kids and schooling. Some parents are currently complaining about the de-tracking policies at the local public high school. They are saying that their brilliant children deserve to be challenged, to enter into the competitive world on equal footing with the rest of the competitive people around.

JULIA: I just do not want to encourage my students to close any doors. We talk a lot about the importance of preparing themselves for as many things as possible. That way, they will not have to go quite so far to pursue something they love later on.

JOE: But going that extra distance to pursue something that you love makes you grow. I say shut the door. Shut all the doors. But understand that this is a choice you are making and take responsibility for it. That does not mean the door is forever shut, unless you get a felony. Felonies shut a lot of doors, so stay within the parameter of those laws. But the process of finding doors when they are ready and figuring out how to open them is so meaningful for students. I did not even get my GED until I was twenty-nine years old. But as I look back on my life, I have a great sense of accomplishment about what I have been able to do. My high school art teachers would say, "Joe, you are not really an artist," but in my heart, I knew I was. Now I have my master of fine arts degree and occasionally sell a sculpture for five thousand bucks. So if kids choose to shut a door and later decide they want to go through it, it is all the more rewarding to accomplish that. And anyone can accomplish it; they just have to understand how to do it and follow through. I try not to give up on kids when I see them heading down a path of academic failure, but there is only so much we can do.

CONNIE: It is interesting how much the institutions in which we teach influence possibilities for teaching and learning. I mean, Margaret, I have watched you hold your students to high expectations and push them to take responsibility for their actions. I think if people knew your teaching, you could get away with having really honest discussions about college and the sorting and sifting that goes on in our society. But we live in a city and state with a lot of institutionalized racism. I just learned that external observers of a local elementary school found school-wide discriminatory treatment of African-American male students.

PAUL: The statistics for African-American high school graduation and incarceration rates in this state are really depressing.[1]

JOE: Oftentimes, because teachers do not want to go outside their box and see that a kid responds to a different teaching style or learns a different way, they perceive that kid as dumb and do not give him the time of day. Through my work with a racial healing group, where we dialogue about the harmful effects of racism, I realized how often African-American males are falling through the cracks at my school and how important it is to recognize that.[2]

Actually, black kids did not take my classes for a long time. They were afraid of me. I represented an Other that they were not used to. If anyone is guilty of stereotyping Indians, man, my black students really did not have a clue. "Do you live in a tepee, Joe?" "Have you ever scalped anyone?" When I finally got these kids to take my classes, that was my wake-up call. I have to connect very differently with these kids. But our staff is resistant to looking at race issues. They think we're doing fine because we have an antiracist mission, but we need to examine ourselves.

CONNIE: It does not make it easier that you are one of two teachers of color at your school. This conversation reminds me of our recent discussion, Joe, about some of your students zoning out in the class on Paul Loeb's book.[3]

JOE: A third of the class, which includes five African-American students, signed up because other classes were full. Unfortunately, over ninety-five percent of the reading completely went over their heads. Usually, we would read and discuss the essays in class and rather than say, "Joe, I don't understand," some kids chose to act out, meaning I had to manage the classroom rather than facilitate discussions. Additionally, the students put minimal effort into writing answers to questions that tried to connect the essays to the students' lives. I have brought up in staff meetings that some classes are just not appropriate for freshmen or kids with really low skills.

CONNIE: Would changing your instructional methods be a way to engage these students?

JOE: Absolutely. But experimenting and coming up with what works for individuals, even with eighteen kids in the class, becomes quite a juggle.

JULIA: Are kids pretty interested in talking about the social issues that appear in the Loeb book?

JOE: When we talk about U.S. history rather than contemporary issues, the students are often engaged in a very critical way. The majority of kids do not have aspirations of becoming part of the powerful elite—they would not be at my school if they did. A lot of them are politically aware and want to hear something different than praise for the current administration. I do not teach history as the glorification of the nation in its evolution through wars and conquest. This nation was built on the backs of slaves and Indian graves, and I would rather be honest about that than glorify the wars.

If we are talking about more contemporary African-American or Native American issues, however, the white guilt factor plays a little bit stronger. That is never my intention but is sort of a natural by-product of teaching a class that emphasizes an oppressed people's issue. My black students are also uncomfortable and resistant to talking about African-American history. I do not know if that is because it brings up too much pain or if it contradicts how they live and act.

I am actually trying to integrate lessons from the racial healing group into my teaching. The African-American woman who currently teaches my school's required class on discrimination does so in such a way that the students' walls go up. She has been an incredible fighter her whole life and so learned that social justice is about fighting back. But when she teaches, the white kids perceive her as calling them little bigots. I would like to try the racial healing approach, which is gentler, but I think more effective.

CONNIE: I wonder if those of you at the middle school level feel like you can teach about institutionalized forms of oppression that complicate an oppressor-oppressed model. I have been reading Rico Gutstein's book about teaching mathematics for social justice to seventh graders, and his students cannot seem to get beyond individual acts of overt racism.[4] So I am wondering how much age influences their understanding of injustice versus the fact that it has been drilled into their heads from day one that this society is all about the individual. Paul, you talk a lot about issues of power during your discussions of history. Do you have a sense of what your students take away from those conversations?

PAUL: My students are good at reading power in their own lives, but they need guidance when thinking about how power is created, used, and abused. I know that browbeating them about how racist they are turns them off. Middle school kids need to be aware of issues like racism, but I do not think it does any good to barrage white males with the idea that the world is evil because of white men. Addressing racism has to be done sensitively and never with a sense of guilt.

One example of how I address power was a recent discussion about the Earl of Sandwich, who supposedly invented the sandwich. One student said, "I imagine people were eating bread and meat a long time before it got named that." So we talked about how being part of the aristocracy might have allowed the earl to make the sandwich popular, even if he did not invent it. We also talked about how he was not an evil person because he had this thing named after him. Oftentimes, we discuss how people in positions of power do things to keep the power they already have. But even for people like Hitler, who aspired to power rather than started his life with it, I ask the students to think about what motivated him to abuse his power. It is always more complex than just being bad or evil, and I try to talk about that with the kids.

JOE: When I hear kids say, "I was not there. It is not my fault, so we need to stop talking about it," I think it is important to point out that they are absolutely right. Today's world is neither their fault nor that of their grandparents. However, as a result of what did happen, they as white people need to be aware of their privileges and make commitments to finding ways toward equality, not just say that affirmative action is bullshit, which I hear a lot.

Unintentionally Leaving Some Children Behind?

In the class Joe taught on essays by peace activists (Loeb 2004), I immediately noticed that a handful of students, all of whom were students of color and most of whom were African-American, were opting out of classroom discussions. Despite Joe's efforts to link essays by Alice Walker, Nelson Mandela, and Vaclav Havel to the students' personal experiences as well as popular movies and music, the students, when they could get away with it, would stick their headphones into their ears and tune Joe out. In contrast, several other, mostly white students, reminded me of the students in Paul's classroom. They articulated stated their viewpoints, were aware of past and present world events, linked arguments made in the essays to other texts they had read, and were unafraid to challenge Joe's viewpoint when they disagreed with him.

At first, I thought Joe might be confronting the resistance of African-American students to doing school, which authors like Signithia Fordham (1996) describe. She argues, "Among underachieving students, resistance is used as cultural mortar to reclaim, create, and expand African-American humanness" (283). However, when I brought in a video camera on two different days, an African-American student named Marvin let his inner celebrity burst forth and complicated my understanding of

Joe's classroom dynamics. Although I could not film Marvin directly because he had not brought in a signed consent form to be videotaped, he revealed much about his functional literacy as he repeatedly invited me to train the camera on him. On the day that the class read Walker's essay, Marvin was enthusiastic to read aloud. As he read, it became clear that he did not recognize several words and had trouble sounding them out. The fact that he was willing to struggle through this reading in front of his teacher and classmates was a testament to his dual desire to learn and be captured on film.

On the second day of filming, Joe's class was reading Havel's essay. That afternoon, I learned that Marvin knew a lot about American football and the racism his aunts and uncles had faced in the South, but very little about events beyond his immediate experience. A horrific shooting of Amish schoolchildren had just occurred, and Marvin solemnly asked Joe if the Amish were Asians when the class discussed this tragedy.[5] After Joe explained who the Amish were, Marvin saved face by jokingly attributing their demise to the fact that Amish adolescents were not allowed to have boyfriends. His lack of knowledge about current events stood in stark contrast to one of the white female students in the class who had clearly read up on both the shooting and the scandal surrounding Representative Mark Foley's inappropriate instant messaging to congressional pages. In that moment, I saw how Paul and Margaret's classrooms had converged in Joe's space—some students came to Park High School with the functional literacy needed to breeze through high school and excel at college, whereas others struggled with basic reading and writing skills, despite the sophisticated oral and compensatory skills they had developed to survive the school day. Not incidental to this conversation is the arrest of Marvin a few weeks after I filmed Joe's class. He did not return to school for the rest of the quarter.

Unfortunately, I did not see Joe work with students on the building of complex reading and writing competencies. The tacit expectation seemed to be that students should come to his class able and willing to read, discuss, and write responses to high-level essays. I knew Joe's philosophy was that he could not make students commit to academic achievement, as the study group's previous conversation makes clear. However, when I was in his classroom I remembered Gloria Ladson-Billing's statement about successful teachers of African-American students: "Students were not permitted to choose failure in their classrooms. [Teachers] cajoled, nagged, pestered, and bribed the students to work at high intellectual levels" (1995, 479).

Joe did try to engage students in academic work by offering them culturally relevant avenues for completing assignments. During the class in which the students read Alex Haley's (1964) *The Autobiography of Malcolm X*, for example, Joe encouraged a student who was an enthusiastic rap artist to create a performance for the final project and hand in lyrics in lieu of a paper. However, I rarely saw Joe work directly with students on assignments, despite his coaxing of them to get to work. When the students were not reading and discussing texts as a group, they worked independently, and Joe by and large remained at his desk.

I do not want to underestimate Joe's consistent efforts to help students analyze injustice and "see themselves as potential social change agents" (Gutstein 2006, 104). I also do not want to minimize the important connections that Joe made with his students, a point I elaborate in chapter six. However, given contemporary U.S. society, with its valorization of standardized test scores, students who do not come to school armed with academic competencies need to learn significantly more in the classroom than how to participate in an engaging conversation about sweatshops if they are to succeed academically. So long as high-level functional literacy translates into economic capital in our society, teachers committed to a more egalitarian society cannot avoid striving to develop it (Olneck 2000). As Ladson-Billings writes, "No matter how good a fit develops between home and school culture, students must achieve. No theory or pedagogy can escape this reality" (1995, 475).

On a related note, Paul's previously mentioned depiction of parental involvement in his school affairs exposes how affluent and well-educated family members can undermine educators' attempts to teach for social justice. Indeed, these parents can and do mobilize their social and political capital in ways that advantage their children, academically and economically, more than "other people's children" (Delpit 1995; Olneck 2000). In our current society, money can buy important educational assets, like private tutoring lessons and trips to see the historical and cultural monuments that appear in school textbooks. Additionally, parents who are well versed in the "culture of power" (Delpit 1995) know how to fight successfully for forms of education that seemingly benefit their children and their children alone, as was the case with the parent group opposing de-tracking measures at Grover High School. Solitary schools and teachers' efforts to diminish social inequality via critical literacy will have limited effects unless or until we collectively decide not to leave anyone behind in our society.

Fortunately, the teachers in this study consistently strove to put student human needs above profit and communal well-being alongside that of the individual. Before turning to this more hopeful part of the story, I feel compelled to address Joe's comment about the "fat gay kid" getting all the attention in his school.

How Does the "Fat Gay Kid" Fit into Critical Literacy?

In the previous dialogue, Margaret's statement about race and class being some of the "biggest" social justice issues strikes me as both true and dangerous. On the one hand, Margaret faces the "gut-wrenching daily constants" of "economic and educational tragedy and pain" (Anyon 2006, 25) in her school setting. Even culturally responsive teaching and critical literacy cannot topple the systemic economic inequality and institutionalized racism that her students currently face. On the other hand, speaking of some injustices as "bigger" than others risks trivializing forms of oppression that cause many people to suffer. Although qualitatively different than the suffering that poverty and racial discrimination cause, the suffering that the "fat gay kid" experiences often leads to the same end: the destruction of human dignity and, at times, life. If, in the tradition of Paolo Freire, critical pedagogy is supposed to emancipate oppressed groups of people, we cannot erase the intersections of gender, race, power, and privilege in our talk about social justice (Meiners and Quinn 2007, 28; Kumashiro 2008). Indeed, intra-school coalitions made up of "students and teachers who are broadly concerned with ... multiple forms of oppression, such as institutional racism, poverty, and heterosexism" are necessary to make urban schools more effective and safe for all students (McCready 2005, 194).

Divesting oneself from the status quo requires understanding the history and expression of hatred toward multiple minority cultures, which cannot occur if some social injustices remain part of the "*null curriculum*" (what is not taught) (Finnessy 2007, 4, emphasis in original). Importantly, calling someone a "fag" was not permitted in Joe's school, where students and staff enforced a strict anti–verbal harassment policy, the effects of which I discuss further in chapter eight. It was in Paul and his co-teacher's classroom, however, where I saw the most intentional teaching of gender identity and sexuality issues. Indeed, they transcended the prohibition of certain terms in their classroom by teaching students *why* such speech was undesirable.

More specifically, a one-on-one conversation with a teacher and student almost always followed a speech offense. These inquiry-based rather than punitive discussions gave students an opportunity to examine their reasons for using a name like "fag" and, in turn, identify taken-for-granted notions of gender and sexuality. They also helped students understand how such language impaired *their,* not just Paul's, learning community. Paul and his co-teacher also made sexuality and gender identity issues an explicit part of the curriculum. Students read and discussed texts like *Am I Blue?* (Bauer 1994), a book of short stories for young adults about lesbian and gay issues, and interacted with LGBTQ (lesbian, gay, bisexual, transgendered, queer, and/or questioning) speakers during their health, wellness, and human sexuality unit.

Unfortunately, this comprehensive approach to addressing body, gender identity, and sexuality issues was unique in my study. In Julia's and Margaret's classrooms, particularly, I heard many derisive comments about females and femininity (by male students) and LGBTQ youth (by all students) but rarely heard teachers or students interrupt them. This lack of intervention allowed "official silence" (Mayo 2004) toward misogyny and heterosexism to flourish. It is worrisome that such expressions of speech remain acceptable as calls for "recuperative masculinity agendas" (Younger and Warrington 2006, 613) multiply. These agendas, which include many single-sex school proposals, often rest on ill-founded, biological assumptions about the differences between boys' and girls' learning styles. Moreover, public outcries about boys' academic failure that ignore complex intersections of race, class, gender, sexuality, nationality, ability, and religion hinder schools' ability to address problematic speech, like "That's so gay" and "You're such a girl," or the deeper issues of which they are a mere symptom.

Student comments associating femininity with weakness and masculinity with dominance clearly reflect prevailing values in our society, which teachers can only do so much to change. Additionally, I want to acknowledge the near absence of institutional arrangements in Julia's and Margaret's school settings to disrupt and transform students' sexist and heterosexist speech and actions (Mayo 2004). In many respects, it is unfair to compare Paul's classroom, where parental and administrative buy-in for addressing gender identity and sexuality issues existed, to Margaret's and Julia's. Nevertheless, I appreciated seeing sexual orientation and gender identity treated as the taught curriculum in his classroom. As Patrick Finnessy asserts, teachers must "give themselves permission to 'teach' to diverse groups of students in a more generous and expansive way to give audible voice to the words 'gay' and 'lesbian' and not let the silent, subtle messages always speak for themselves or go unheard" (2007, 5).

Conclusion

> A truly anti-oppressive education should not entail an individual over-coming of oppressive tendencies by rationally talking about the problem to make it go away. I am reminded of Goldenberg's (1992) analysis showing how the self-fulfilling prophecy—the "expectancy effect"—had more to do with what teachers actually did (or did not do) than with anything teachers expected of their students. Likewise, a truly anti-oppressive education ... should be focused on the very ways we have constructed how we go about teaching and learning.
>
> —*Dan Butin, "This Ain't Talk Therapy"*

Thus far, this book has attempted to show the importance of functional, skills-based instruction for students whose access to the "culture of power" (Delpit 1995) has been historically thwarted. It has also emphasized that succeeding academically "in the traditional sense" may open doors for students but does not necessarily help them challenge inequitable institutions or power relations (Gutstein 2006, 30). Such resistance requires critical literacy.

However, as Butin's (2002) quote emphasizes, students need to do more than learn how to rationally talk about oppression if they are to disrupt it in long-term, meaningful ways. In other words, the imparting of critical knowledge, though significant, is inadequate to the task of building a better social order. Even a more robust vision of critical literacy, which includes developing a deeper understanding of sociopolitical issues, taking a stand on those issues, analyzing multiple perspectives, and being able to name and identify injustices when they arise, presents only strands of the complicated web that constitutes education for social justice. To leave the story here would thus reinforce a limited, linear model of education for social justice, with functional and critical literacies on opposite ends of the spectrum.

Admittedly, the assumption that students need a certain level of functional literacy before they can effectively challenge systemic injustices underlay many of our study group discussions. However, our discussions and my observations of the teachers' classrooms revealed contradictions in this neat stage theory. After all, we also discussed the potential educational value of making students uncomfortable—regardless of their functional or critical literacy levels—through experiential, arts-based, and risk-taking activities. Additionally, this dual literacy model does not adequately capture the development of additional competencies for social justice that require more than a bundle of knowledge and skills. These competencies include cultivating solidarity, working through difficult emotions (like shame, fear, and guilt), and publicly acting up—that is, directly challenging the status quo—when called for. Deep-seated dispositions toward social justice rarely if ever emerge from the efficient, scientific planning of people (Popkewitz 2006). Indeed, I have yet to meet someone who learned solely through textbook knowledge or conscious reasoning the courage to dissent publicly, the humility to examine continuously one's own blind spots, or the ability to witness "the physical, material, and psychological suffering of others, to put ourselves 'inside the skin' of the other" (Nhat Hanh 1992, 81).

Instead, poignant experiences and interpersonal relationships often incite people to work collectively for a more just and peaceful world. In the remaining pages, I discuss additional practices that the teachers undertook to destabilize narrow, technical constructions of teaching and learning and cultivate in their students what I call relational, democratic, and visionary literacies.

PART III

RELATIONAL LITERACY

5

Relational Literacy in Context

A Portrait of Julia

(Julia's responses to the portrait appear in italics.)
The wind was gusting and the sky a dull gray the first January morning
I drove to Hancock. The Hobson landscape of fast food restaurants and
apartment buildings quickly gave way to fallow fields and barren clusters
of trees as the city street turned into a highway. Located about ten miles
from Hobson's center, Hancock was a small town of fewer than eighty-
five hundred people. The town's welcome sign, posted near the highway
exit, celebrated the state championship of the high school boys' soccer
team several years earlier.

Julia agreed to participate in my study but not without reservation.
For four years, she had been teaching in the Reach Program, designed
for high school students who were doing poorly in school. She was thus
nervous about her beginner teacher status and my observation of her
classroom. I tried to reassure her that I would be observing to learn about
her teaching context—not to evaluate her instruction—and would give
her feedback on my observations whenever she wanted it. We both knew,
however, that I needed to be physically present in her classroom before
my pat guarantees would amount to something more than words.

When I entered the large brick building that housed about a thousand
students, I was surprised at how welcoming it felt. The high school had been
renovated within the last ten years, and, as a result, its drab concrete was
transformed into bright hues, the cafeteria into an open-space commons.
Circling the rows of cafeteria tables were food counters, administrative

offices, and a student services area. With its high ceilings, bustling activity, and paintings of the high school's mascot (a tiger) and mission statement ("Work together for success while learning to live respectfully and responsibly in a changing world"), this area was the community's center.

Three female students were self-consciously announcing senior awards (such as "best dressed" and "worst car") over the loud speaker as I waited for Julia in the main office. Once she found me, Julia led me through the maze of hallways to her classroom, at the periphery of the building. As we navigated a pathway among the students scurrying to their next class, Julia explained to me the Reach Program's setup. The principal allocated two rooms for the program: a resource lab with computers where students could hang out and study, and a classroom where freshmen took a study skills class and sophomores a guided study hall, both for credit. During the nine-period day, Julia and her co-teacher divvied up the responsibilities of running the program. They each staffed the resource lab for three periods as well as taught two study skills classes and a guided study class.

Julia was also the case manager for approximately forty Reach Program students. She characterized this role as "making sure kids don't get lost in the shuffle." As a case manager, she provided additional support to the students that the overextended counselors and teachers couldn't—namely, monitoring students' academic progress; liaising teachers, administrators, and parents to improve the students' chances of academic achievement; and giving the students additional academic help. When we reached her classroom door, Julia informed me that once the spring semester began, she would also begin co-teaching a "pre-pre-algebra" course for students who had already failed algebra two or more times.

Two things caught my eye as I entered Julia's classroom: the numerous student photos on the whiteboard at the front of the room, hanging from a mobile, and next to Julia's desk, and a wooden bookshelf near the door that connected the classroom to the resource lab. The latter housed many young adult books that I recognized from my own experiences as a high school and teacher educator. Among them were *Monster, Maus,* and *Nickel and Dimed.*[1] I later learned that Julia bought these books or had them donated. I also noticed two computers against the back wall and nine standard school-issued metal and Formica-topped desks filling the rest of the room. Before I could explore the resource lab, two students arrived for class and began gushing to Julia—Ms. Goldberg—about another student's recent breakup with her boyfriend.

Finding Julia

"Julia's out back playing volleyball," Amber said after greeting me by the bar with a beer. "I told her you wanted to meet and ask her about participating in your study." Dingy and dark, this local dive was famous for its hamburgers and, during the warmer months, its volleyball league. Teams played on the outdoor sand court behind the bar. I followed Amber through the crowd toward the back door and realized I was about to introduce myself to a potential research participant while holding a plastic cup of beer in my hand. I set it down on a table near the exit.

I first heard about Julia while describing my research project to Amber, right after we began dating in October 2006. When I told her my plan was to recruit four teachers who identified themselves as teaching for social justice, she replied, "You might want to talk to Julia. I think she teaches math in Hancock, and this study seems like it would be right up her alley."

This information was all I had to go on as I entered the bar's courtyard. Amber pointed to a woman about my age with curly brown hair and glasses who was sitting in the bleachers next to the volleyball court. As we approached her, Amber said, "Julia, Connie. Connie, Julia. I'm gonna let you two talk." Before either of us could say anything, Amber was gone.

"Hi, Julia. I'm not sure what Amber already told you, but … "

"She said you are working on an educational research project and mentioned something about social justice."

"That's the gist of it. I'm trying to find four teachers who consider themselves to be working for social justice and form a," I paused, "research study group." How on earth was I going to sell my project in this setting? "Amber said you teach math at the high school level down in Hancock?"

"I'm certified in math, but I actually run a program for 'at-risk' kids. We changed its name to the Reach Program to fight against some of the negativity associated with 'at-risk,' but the program is basically for freshmen and sophomores who are struggling to pass their classes and stay in school." My ears perked up. Not only did her description of what she did have obvious links to social justice issues, but she also would add the voice of a teacher who was trying to help kids succeed in school more generally (as opposed to teaching them a discrete subject area, like geometry or U.S. history).

"I know this is not the ideal place to talk about work," I said. "Any chance you would be willing to meet me for coffee to talk about my project and your potential participation in it?"

"Sure, but I'm not sure I qualify as a teacher of social justice," Julia replied.

"That's okay. The more teachers I talk to, the more I realize that they don't usually use this language." As these words tumbled out of my mouth, I realized I was going to have to justify this newly sprouted decision to the overseers of my study, as I had emphasized that the study participants would self-identify as teaching for social justice in my research proposal.

"Can I give you a call or e-mail you, Julia?"

"Sure, do you have something to write my e-mail address down on?"

"Be right back." I reentered the bar, grabbed a napkin, and asked the bartender if I could borrow a pen. Moments later, I procured Julia's contact information and, potentially, her willingness to be the first recruit of my research project.

A Day in the Life of Julia

Julia's typical school day could and did include meeting with a student's foster mom and social worker, negotiating the special education status of a student who had been homeschooled until his freshman year of high school and, as a result, needed more resources than the Reach Program could provide, and persuading a student that her personal vendetta against an English teacher was not in her long-term best interest. As Julia said about her job, "You're more involved in the bigger picture—their schooling and their lives beyond school walls—than a regular classroom teacher. When you have a ton of kids in, say, a math class, you have to keep a certain amount of distance or you'll just get consumed. In my position, it's part of your job to get consumed."

When the spring semester started in late January 2006, Julia modified her study skills class. The second half of each class period remained the same: Students worked on assignments from other classes, and Julia helped them as needed. She also ensured that the students had filled out their academic planners. Provided by Julia, the planners were supposed to foster students' organizational skills and help them set realizable academic goals. During the first half of the class, on the other hand, the students no longer learned discrete skills like note-taking. Rather, they practiced more general literacy skills by reading and writing about books of their own choosing.

Throughout the third quarter, the first twenty minutes of most class periods was devoted to Julia or the students reading aloud a book that they selected as a class, such as *How to Be a Successful Criminal.*[2] During the fourth quarter, the students spent the first half of the period silently reading and writing paragraph-long reactions to individually chosen books. Julia read alongside the students and brought in a rug and bean-bag from home, on which the students could sprawl out while they read. She also set weekly reading goals with them, which she tracked on a faux bookshelf posted on the classroom wall. When they collectively reached three thousand pages, she rewarded them with a pizza party. Although several students initially resisted these reading activities, as time wore on, I noticed that the distracting noises and complaints waned, and noses remained buried in books throughout the silent reading period. Most of the students seemed to like reading after all.

One day of the week, Julia took a break from extolling the virtues of reading and writing and nurtured her passion for service learning. The idea of incorporating community service into the Reach Program came to Julia during her first year at Hancock High School. At that time, the program still included juniors. "When I walked in," Julia said, "all of the students who had improved their academic achievement were pushed out of the program by their junior year. So the juniors I did have were the kinds of kids who walked in the door and said, 'There's no fucking way I'm working for you.'" She decided that tutoring elementary students might be one activity that the students would not refuse to do. Having placed each junior in a different classroom, Julia found that the students thrived in these settings. "The elementary kids thought their tutors were cool because they were clearly the badasses at the high school," she said. "And my students responded much better to these kids who were looking up to them than to any of their teachers." As for Julia, "Tutoring kind of saved the whole year for me."

By the time I met Julia in the fall of 2005, the juniors were gone from the Reach Program, but she had instituted a weekly volunteer activity for the freshman study skills class. Therefore, on Wednesdays her students left campus to work with either senior citizens at a local retirement home or elementary students in surrounding schools. At the former, the students interacted with characters like Bill, a seventy-something-year-old who had stitches across his eyebrow and a balding, freckled head. Bill had served in the navy in Vietnam right before the war broke out and loved having a young audience with whom to share his colorful stories about South Asia and the subsequent twenty-five years, when he was a bodybuilder and natural food restaurant owner in California. As they talked with the residents, the students had to confront their fears of the elderly in a society obsessed with youthfulness. They also could not help but perceive the seniors' palpable appreciation of their visits. Upon entering the senior center on a blustery winter morning, for example, I overheard the residents chatter excitedly about the students' visit. The students broke up the loneliness and tedium of their daily lives.

At the elementary schools, the students worked in a variety of class-rooms. One high school student volunteered for the speech and language program, and another, who had expressed interest in becoming an artist, was placed with an art teacher. On the bus ride back to the high school campus, the students jabbered about the funny things the kids had said and the various tasks the teachers had them do, from grading papers to playing indoor hockey. I knew the experience was meaningful for them when Brittany, a student with an infinite appetite for complaining, said, "That wasn't so bad."

Julia emphasized that this weekly volunteering opportunity only fulfilled the community service aspect of her service learning philosophy. Her dream, in contrast, was to integrate community service and academic learning. She wanted to create a class wholly devoted to a service project that the students selected, proposed, researched, and carried out. Still, for many of the students who felt they were "in the dumb class," the Wednesday community service activities created an opportunity for them to feel like valuable and contributing members of the larger Hancock community.

Prior to Becoming a Teacher ...

"So I grew up in New York and Connecticut," Julia told me as she settled onto the sofa next to the crackling fire. We decided to do the interview in Julia's home, a two-story craftsman-style house that Julia had been reno-vating on her own. She held a sheet of paper with my tentative interview questions on it and was in the process of describing her childhood.

"We lived in Ossining," Julia continued, "a mixed-class New York suburb about an hour outside of the city. Then, when I was in eighth grade, my mom remarried. My parents got divorced when I was eight and, right before I started high school, she married a man who lived in Connecticut. So my sisters and I followed my mom and stepfather to this Connecticut commuter town. It was very wealthy and very white. When I graduated from high school, I moved to Hobson for college and have been here ever since."

"Was religion an important part of your ... " Julia's large boxer, Adam, began whimpering on the floor near my feet.

"He would be happiest if he could come up and sit with you," Julia said, motioning to Adam with her hand. As he leaped up on the couch, Julia answered my unfinished question. "I went to Hebrew school once it was time to be bat mitzvahed, not when I was young. My grandmother went to temple pretty regularly, and my dad had gone as a kid, but my mom never went. So I guess Hebrew school was kind of an afterthought. Once we had our bat mitzvah parties, however, my time at the temple was pretty much done."

"Does your family celebrate the Jewish holidays pretty regularly?" I asked.

"My sisters and I do. I would say we go to temple for the high holidays, like Rosh Hashanah and Yom Kippur, most of the time."

"And what do your parents do?"

"My mom is a psychiatric social worker. She was actually a teacher until we were born but then stopped working to raise us. She went back to school to become a social worker after my parents split up."

"And your father?"

"My dad is a doctor. I think he got his M.D. right after we were born."

"Does that mean your mom helped him get through med school?"

"My mom's parents paid for him—paid for him to go and lost the money in the divorce. Ooooh!" Julia laughed and twisted her mouth into an expression of exaggerated pain.

I hoped I had not hit a nerve with my question. "What did you get your undergraduate degree in?" I asked, trying to steer the conversation away from family issues.

"History and Italian."

"I know you did construction work for a while after college. Was that right after you graduated, or did you do something else first?"

"That was the first thing I did after college," Julia responded. "I was toying with the idea of being an architect since there are a lot of architects in my family, but I discovered that architects had too much desk work. So I progressed to the idea that I wanted to build things and, after I graduated, went to work for a construction company to see what I could learn and do.

"Unfortunately, the guy for whom I worked ran into some financial issues," Julia continued. "When he stopped paying me after six months, I started doing woodworking. I got this idea in my head that I wanted to be a woodworker in New York. So I went to a cabinetmaking program at the local community college for a year." Julia stopped to take a breath. Then Julia described her epiphany:

> I went and worked for this shop
> out in Dodgetown.
> Nutty owners who sold pretty high-end, pricey stuff.
> All custom cabinetry and custom furniture—
> the clients were so demanding.
>
> I just got in this zone,
> this crisis:
> Why am I doing this?
> Does this work even matter?
> Why am I investing so much emotional energy
> in this job?
> And the other piece—
> where is the pleasure in this
> for me?
>
> This one weird day
> all the machines were on.
> It was really loud;
> I had earmuffs on;
> I hadn't talked to anyone all day.
> I was all worked up
> about something not fitting right.
> I thought,
> this is not worth it.
>
> I'm going to be a teacher.

Contextualizing Hancock and the Reach Program

Scratching Adam behind the ears, I asked Julia, "So what is your current educational setting like, not only within your program but also in the school as a whole? You know, who are the students? What are the other teachers and your principal like? All that kind of stuff."

"You want me to dish on my whole school?" she replied.

I laughed, and Julia began describing the town. "It's a pretty mixed community. You know it's a bedroom community for Hobson, so there are a fair number of people who commute there to work. While you have this cross-section of well-educated, more affluent types, you also have people whose families have grown up in Hancock and lived there for generations. A lot of them are farmers and pretty darn white. Hancock's changing, though. In the four years I've been there, the Hispanic population has grown. There are also tiny African-American and Hmong populations as well as this chunk of kids from foster homes. I would say that half to three-quarters of the black kids in our school are in foster placements. It's pretty rare for them to be at Hancock High School for all four years."

"Do these foster teens usually find their way into the Reach Program?"

"Mmm hmm," Julia confirmed. "If you look at the students of color in our school and the programs they're in, it's a little alarming. The number of students of color in the Reach Program is way disproportionate when looking at the demographics of the entire school."

"Didn't you also say that there is only one teacher of color in the school?"

"In the district," Julia replied.

"In the entire district, there's only one teacher of color!?" This far exceeded the eighty-seven percent that I had read represented the proportion of white teachers in K–12 education nationally.[3] "Well what are your fellow teachers like for the most part?" I asked. "Do you find that you have a different view of the world than they do?"

"Definitely," Julia nodded. "But I agree with something my principal said a long time ago: Putting together a team of people with different ideas actually strengthens the team. Plus, I know that different students respond to different teachers according to their needs. In any case, we have some very traditional teachers and some teachers that should have been fired a long time ago," Julia said, laughing.

"Are there a fair amount of new teachers, too?"

"There's always a lot of new, young teachers. We have huge numbers of retirements, which is partly a baby boomer thing. But I feel like there are a lot of teachers who have been at the high school their entire career."

"Do you have a sense that the newer teachers, by virtue of having gone through teacher training recently, have similar perspectives as you on education and teaching?"

"I guess, but even among the newer teachers who have been exposed to similar philosophies, there's variation in how teachers do things. And teachers have a lot of flexibility to do their own thing."

"Because of your principal?" I asked.

Julia shook her head affirmatively.

"From other comments you've made to me, it seems like your principal is very supportive of you—"

"I love my principal," Julia interrupted. "Actually, I like all three of my principals. But our big principal," Julia laughed at the image her words conjured. "Our main principal, that is, really believes in letting teachers find their own way and do what works best for them. As far as my program goes, probably ninety-nine percent of the time he's said, 'yes,' when I've made requests."

"What kinds of requests have you made?" I asked.

"Well, with the off-campus tutoring stuff, he said, 'No problem.' And two years ago he basically gave us the science department's computer lab, which they barely used. That's our current resource lab."

"With all the recent state budget cuts in education, is money a problem?"

"Money hasn't been an issue, which is dreamy," Julia replied.

"Wow! That's not something I hear too often." Hoping to hear more about her students, I asked, "So you talked a little bit about your students' race and ethnicity. How else would you characterize the students that you have in the Reach Program?"

"I kind of categorize the students in terms of who they are and what their needs are," Julia responded as she got up to put more wood on the fire. "Usually I see a big split between the types of students who are referred to my program. I would say that about a quarter of the kids need additional support, time, and skill development but don't qualify for special ed. Those are the kids for whom the study skills curriculum is really valuable, and they, well, they learn it, they participate, and they do it. And," Julia laughed as she returned to the couch, "I hope the curriculum's useful. Then, I would say seventy-five percent of the kids are the kids who have stuff going on in their lives that's more important than school, whether it's a difficult home life, their peers, or drugs and alcohol. They're disengaged from their education."

"When you mentioned tough home lives, it made me wonder how many of your students are facing social class issues at and beyond school."

"Some of our kids are definitely facing rural poverty. There are real disparities in terms of where the kids are coming from and what kind of money their families have. But the interesting thing is that you see all kinds of students in my program."

"Do you think sexuality at all influences—"

"Who is in my program?" Julia finished the question for me.

"Yeah, I mean is homophobia an issue that's even discussed in your school?" I asked.

"It comes up," Julia replied. "We have a Gay-Straight Alliance, and I have a few students who are pretty active in it. But I don't think sexuality usually has much to do with why kids come into my program." *Thinking on this issue as I read the portrait, I have had two "out" students come through the program in four years (out of about one hundred), although we certainly have some budding homosexual students in the mix. I just have to imagine that an increased likelihood of isolation and depression, which are common characteristics among my students, is a pretty strong undercurrent for those LGBT students.*

"Mainly, I think of my students as the ones for whom the system is not working. And, basically, our solution is to give them more of the same— make it more intense and give them more of it. I mean my students have more support, and that helps. But it is hard to see how we are changing the system for them. So that's a struggle."

POSTSCRIPT: I failed to ask Julia about the gender breakdown of her students, despite my ongoing interest in how sexism is sustained and resisted in classrooms as well as the recent media hoopla over the ways in which the education system is failing boys. So as not to omit gender issues in this section, I want to acknowledge here that Julia's two freshman study skills classes had approximately three female students for every male student in the fall, which dropped to two female students for every male student in the spring.

Racialized Conflict in Julia's Classroom

After several visits to Julia's study skills classes, I started to notice some troubling things. Although several of the students would pull out their history or math textbooks when they had work time, other students refused to do anything, disrupted other students, tried to sneak onto the Internet, or agreed to do only nonacademic activities, like help Julia cut out laminated images for classroom displays. Although this behavior was not in and of itself worrying—high school students, after all, often demonstrate their power by refusing to "do school"—the fact that the bulk of students who repeatedly resisted doing intellectual work were African-American was. Additionally, Julia was going to battle almost daily with one of her African-American students, Kasha, who was struggling both in and outside school.

In general, Julia had a collegial relationship with her students that involved a lot of joking and playful interactions. She had a seemingly limitless supply of patience and spent however much time was needed to explain something to a student in a way that she or he could understand. The students frequently divulged aspects of their personal lives to Julia, demonstrating their considerable trust in her. Additionally, she often had food on hand for hungry students and offered academic help to students during her planning periods and beyond school hours. Of course the students occasionally had bad days. At these times, Julia pulled aside students for one-on-one talks about the reasons underlying their disruptive behavior. Usually, however, Julia worked out conflicts with students in private, without much ado.

Not so with Kasha. If Julia did not allow her to have her way, Kasha did everything in her power to create a scene. One day, for example, Kasha came into class complaining about an eye problem and asked Julia if she could go to the nurse. Julia permitted her to leave, but Kasha resumed chasing, jabbing, and joking with her peers until Julia pleaded with her to go. *Pleading, huh? Not as in charge as I hope I am, I guess . . .*

Kasha returned fifteen minutes later and, to evade Julia's questions about why she did not have a pass from the nurse, started talking to a fellow student. Julia tried to get the class back on track by saying, "We're really struggling with students' coming and going. It's really distracting for everyone. When you come in, it would be nice if you just got your stuff and sat down."

Kasha retorted, "I know you're just talking to me, Ms. Goldberg."

"No, you are one of the people I'm talking to," Julia replied, "but you're not everyone." Kasha proceeded to shove all of her books and notebooks onto the floor, and Julia asked her to leave. Kasha resumed conversation with her friends, forcing Julia to implore her departure once again until Kasha was finally out the door.

Situations like these led to a meeting in which Julia, Kasha, and the principal cowrote a behavioral contract. If Kasha abided by the contract, she could stay in Julia's class. If not, she would go to a study hall in the student services office by herself. Kasha broke the contract shortly thereafter and was forced to leave Julia's study skills class.

Concerned about her souring relationship with Kasha, Julia asked me in mid-February if I had any resources or feedback that might make her more effective with her students. In addition to suggesting some books and videos related to race, ethnicity, and racism that Julia could use on her own or with her students (such as *The Color of Fear, Race: The Power of an Illusion,* and *Because of the Kids*), I started sending my field notes to Julia.[4] I also suggested that she speak with Margaret, the other white female teacher in the study, who, unlike me, was a veteran teacher, had been a foster parent for ten years, and predominantly taught African-American students.

Around the same time that Julia removed Kasha from the study skills class, her relationship with another African-American student, Deondra, became increasingly conflict ridden. The more that Julia tried to engage her, the more Deondra resisted. On one April afternoon, after Julia asked Deondra to put her cell phone away and get to work on her environmental science project, Deondra pulled out a cosmetics bag and began applying makeup. When Julia told her to put it away, Deondra replied, "Ms. Goldberg just won't leave me alone!"

Julia teased, "I know! What is my problem? I won't let you sit there and do nothing."

"I hate you!" Deondra punched back in a loud voice.

I had just heard a speaker from an after-school Afrocentric program when this interaction occurred, and told Julia that if she was interested, I could share my notes and the resources mentioned at this talk, such as the book *Black Students: Middle Class Teachers.*[5] Julia said she would like to talk about changing the dynamic with Deondra, and we ended up meeting at a restaurant during an evening toward the end of April. Julia's decision to place herself in the vulnerable position of learner was not surprising. From the moment we met, she expressed a desire to challenge herself and improve her teaching. As she said in the December interview about her reasons for agreeing to participate in the study:

> The big thing for me is that I struggle to feel like I'm being effective, like I'm doing the best I can for my students. I need to feel like I'm constantly growing and working toward improvement. I don't want to burn out, you know, because my job can be really difficult and frustrating. So I think as long as I feel like I'm getting better at teaching, I'm going to be happy and feel good about what I'm doing. I really want to stay focused on being conscious about what I'm doing in the classroom and about making positive changes.

During our discussion at the restaurant, we walked the tricky tightrope of cultural competence, trying to balance historical social patterns with individual differences. Having noticed that most of the African-American students in Margaret's class responded immediately and positively when she called them out on disruptive behavior in front of the class, for example, I asked Julia if she thought greater public acknowledgment of troubling behavior might be more effective than pulling students aside and speaking with them one-on-one. Julia saw this option as potentially leading to more conflict and backlash, and I did not push further. After all, I had only been with these students about a dozen times, whereas Julia saw them every day and had developed a meaningful relationship with each of them. Moreover, I was no more an insider in these African-American teens' lives than Julia was. The particular issues in Julia's classroom required context-specific remedies, but we could not ignore the more global reality faced by Julia's students of color who came into class saying things like, "There are racist people in this school," and, "If you were in my position, you wouldn't want to do any work either."

We did not come up with any long-term solutions to the teacher-student conflicts in Julia's classroom that night, but she and her students ended the school year on a positive note. She and several students raised money for and participated in a five-kilometer race for breast cancer research during the first week of June. Deondra walked the entire thing in flip-flops, and Kasha traveled to the race in Julia's car. En route, Julia overheard Kasha and another student discussing her new foster placement, about which Kasha was hopeful, even though the move would require transferring to another school and making a new set of friends. *I think it was a really tough year for Deondra at home, and I actually think she realized that she was going to miss me. She did not offer the usual sweetness, given only to manipulate, at the end of the year.*

Like Kasha, Julia would not be coming back to the high school the following year. During the spring semester, she decided to return to her former job as a mathematics teacher. Julia had taught mathematics in the Hancock district as a long-term substitute teacher immediately after obtaining her teaching certification and enjoyed it immensely. She only left the position because a more senior teacher ended up applying for it. When a middle school mathematics position opened up in March, Julia decided to submit an application. She did not attribute this move to the Reach Program students, although I imagine some of Julia's struggles with them influenced her decision to leave the high school. Rather, she had a difficult working relationship with the program's co-teacher and did not see significant improvement on the horizon.

Of course the students are part of it. It is pretty exhausting on an emotional level in so many ways working with these students. So much of what I do involves patience and persistence, but also, hugely, is about force of personality. I don't think that my personality is a strength in this job—I'm just way too uptight. Lisa [the educational assistant] has been a really big influence in helping me relax and have more fun at work, which is reflected in my relationship with my students. The prospect of navigating the program without her, dealing with my co-teacher, and focusing my teaching on Reach Program students doesn't seem feasible. My preference, however, would have been to stay at the high school . . .

There was no doubt in my mind that Julia was fully invested in accompanying her students to the graduation stage and helping them become active, engaged, respected citizens in their communities. By leaving, she was tending to her own well-being. Julia's fund-raising e-mail for the five-kilometer race, sent to her friends and family members, best describes her feelings about and commitment to her students:

I'm in my fourth year working with students who struggle in school (the jargon is "at-risk"). Each student has their own unique set of strengths, talents, needs, and issues that create challenges and opportunities. Like most teenagers, they are a charming, frustrating, risk-taking, attention-seeking bunch. Most of our students are distracted by the circumstances of their lives, which tend to eclipse the relevance of algebra, grammar, and the periodic table. For some students, just making it to school on a daily basis is not a given. Others have moved in and out of the district 3 or more times already ...

This is a great opportunity for a group of teenagers to see beyond themselves and do something that benefits not only their own health, but also instills upon them a sense of civic awareness and ownership of their small community.

Julia's Teaching Philosophy

"Is there anything in particular that you think has influenced your teaching most—an experience, event, social interaction?" I asked toward the end of our interview.

"Well, I think part of it for me is that the whole time I was in high school, I was just so uncomfortable," Julia replied. "I felt stupid and didn't enjoy it."

"Why do you think that was?"

"I was one of those kids who disappeared, you know?"

I nodded, even though I was not one of those kids.

"And I see this now as a teacher," Julia continued. "The kid who slips under the radar for whatever reason. She is perfectly pleasant, seems fairly well adjusted—maybe not particularly delightful or charming—but she's just kind of invisible. I've realized that it wasn't until college that I became more confident as a student. When I went back to school to become a teacher—and I think most people who are returning adults probably sense this—I was suddenly like, 'I'm perfect,'" Julia laughed. "'I've got opinions. I've got things to say. I'm going to express myself, and I don't care what you think.' That was pretty empowering."

"So how do you think your educational experiences have influenced how you teach high school students today?"

"I feel like I know what it's like to be a student in a given moment," Julia replied. "And despite what I just said, I know that school came easily to me, that I excelled at school. But I also know what it's like to really struggle at it from my math certification experience. That was a huge challenge for me."

"I knew you were certified in math and history," I said, "but I guess I assumed that math was one of the areas in which you were always successful."

"Actually, I never liked math," Julia admitted. "My dad's a super math geek. He does math problems in the tub for fun."

I laughed at this image.

"But I never felt good at it or like I understood it," Julia continued. "It also never appealed to me because I'm a creative person, and math never seemed creative. I thought maybe I didn't get the concepts because only math people teach math. So I decided I should be a non-math person who teaches math."

"Did you struggle with the math content classes, then, when you were getting your certification?" I asked.

"Calculus was really hard," Julia confessed. "I didn't even understand what the teacher was talking about when I first returned to math classes, which was five years after taking a single math course as an undergraduate. It was like she was speaking a different language. And the probability class I took—I am probability stupid. I had a couple of experiences in that class where I thought, God, nobody should have to feel like this."

"Like what?"

"Well, when the teacher handed back our first test," Julia answered, "she had listed all the grades on the board, and mine was the lowest one. I got like a forty-two percent or something." Julia winced in mock agony.

"Do you think these experiences helped you connect with the students in the Reach Program?" I asked.

"Yeah," Julia replied. "I do not assume that people get concepts, and I think it made me much more patient in terms of finding four different ways to explain the same thing."

I looked down at the list of questions I had brought to guide the discussion. "I think this conversation is a good segue to another big question. How would you describe your philosophy of teaching?" I asked.

"I guess the biggest thing is that ... " Julia stopped speaking and sighed. "I just feel like our schools are set up in one very specific way and style. For me, my teaching, and my program," she paused. "It's just there are all these students for whom this system does not work. So rather than calling them stupid, prodding them, or flunking them, what can we do? What are our other options to help these students come into their own?

"We've got to work within this environment," she added. "It's the only environment we've got right now. To some extent, these students are always going to be somewhat in the system regardless of who they are or what career paths they choose. So I try to help them get the most out of schooling while still preserving some dignity, self-esteem, and respect."

"Do you have a vision, then, of what an ideal educational experience for K–12 students would be?" I asked.

"God, I just," she paused. "I think it would be awesome if every kid could walk out of school saying, 'I would love to be a teacher,' because school is a place where they felt comfortable, confident, successful, and like they were challenged—that they really grew in that place and were proud of what they did. Every kid should walk out of school feeling proud.

"Come to think of it, I would like to walk out of school feeling proud," she said, laughing.

6

More than "Fluffy Talk"

The Significance of Relational Literacy

At a conference I recently attended, a white male teacher educator referred to the human relations aspects of education for social justice as "fluffy." He went on to say that changing hearts and minds was important but insufficient when systemic issues were ignored. As he spoke, I felt distaste for his expert posturing and looked forward to the next presentation. To my great delight, the subsequent speaker talked about flaunting her queerness in the face of a public shaming of her sexuality. Unfortunately, she felt compelled to begin her presentation by saying she had never imagined standing at the podium to talk about feeling bad. In both speakers' statements, there was an implicit ranking of reason above emotion that has a long, deep, gendered, classed, and racialized history in "Enlightened" countries like the United States (St. Pierre 2000). Although attending solely to the emotional aspects of education for social justice is inadequate, I want to argue in this chapter that teachers' ability to connect emotionally with their students—to care—is critical to a socially just education, which, after all, takes place within and between thinking *and* feeling human beings. In Kathleen Lynch and John Baker's terms, "being cared for is a fundamental prerequisite for mental and emotional well-being and for human development generally" (2005, 133).

I also want to acknowledge up front that relational literacy is a contested concept. Because displays of solidarity can be used to manipulate and control others, especially those over whom we have power, we need to approach caring for others with care. In the world of schooling, particularly, teachers who assign grades and/or determine the classes in which their students will be placed are not on equal footing with their students. Accordingly, teachers' attempts to establish friendship with students may garner their resentment or resistance if students perceive the teacher-student relationship as only superficially reciprocal (Tannen 1986).

Indeed, I avoided "caring" when seeking to label relational literacy because of its significant link to injustice. Unfortunately, calls to "help" or "care for" students often ignore larger social, political, and histori-cal issues (Popkewitz 1998). When teachers' attention becomes wholly focused on ameliorating individual students' "psychological difficulties" (Popkewitz 1998, 67) and thus fails to consider the broader context in which these problems are rooted, teachers may end up pitying rather than empowering students to act collectively for social change. Additionally, when caring teachers do not hold high expectations for their students, they may "feel sorry for 'underprivileged' youth but never challenge them academically" (Katz, in Antrop-González and De Jesús 2006, 426). Moreover, an ethic of caring, although valued by many cultural minority groups, is not validated by "Eurocentric institutions except the family" (Collins, in Ladson-Billings 1994, 156). Thus caring, even when not paternalistic, is frequently relegated to the fluffy world of "private," interpersonal relationships.

The failure to address human relationships in talk about social jus-tice is unacceptable precisely because "public tragedies of social discord and injustice ... are large-scale manifestations of the failure of com-munication that plays itself out in private homes" (Tannen 1986, 193). Our interpersonal relationships influence the ways in which we act and approach others in the world. In education, specifically, when teachers do not recognize the cultural and linguistic assets that their students bring to the classroom, they risk both hindering individual students' academic success and sending the message that respect is reserved for those in positions of power (Valenzuela 1999). What is more, teachers' intentional and unintentional disregard for some students often hinders those students' ability to appreciate "their own value, intelligence, and potential as political actors," which Jean Anyon emphasizes is critical to creating broad-based, transformative social movements (2005, 179).

I address democratic discourse styles that help to resolve cultural misunderstandings in chapter eight; here, I emphasize the need for "a more humane vision of schooling" that includes attention to "students' subjective reality" (Valenzuela 1999, 24, 22). As in previous chapters, I foreground an abridged study group conversation because it reveals important similarities and differences among the teachers' approaches to connecting with students in their diverse educational settings. Then, to bolster my claims, I explore the concept of relational literacy and its connection to education for social justice, drawing on classroom illustrations and educational scholarship on caring.

Attempting to Transform an Authoritarian Culture into a Connected One

JULIA: At the high school, I wanted to learn about my students' experiences—what they believed about themselves—but my assigned mission was to get them across the stage with their diplomas. I had this very structured program that allowed many of them to get through high school, but I wanted to make sure I recognized and appreciated all the things that my students walked into the school with. I did not want the students to perceive me as believing that education is only for white, middle-class students and that they should be striving to act white and middle class.

JOE: But it could be that that was perceived, regardless of your attitude. People oftentimes have to figure out significant life lessons on their own, and, in my own experience, I did not want to be told by a mainstream instructor that schooling was my ticket to success.

JULIA: So what should I have done? They were with me because they had already checked out in most of their classes. There is part of me that thinks you are right and what I said about the importance of education was useless. When your students' parents, whom they love and respect, did not go to college or maybe are in jail, what message do you give them about education? I could not just say, "I have nothing to offer you."

PAUL: Well, what did your students tell you they wanted, or did they have no idea?

JULIA: A lot of kids wanted to be rich without having to work for it. Dealing drugs seemed like a great option for some. Others were very invested in a clear and deliberate "I don't care" attitude. My students had often been told, "You are not effective and cannot have an impact." I worry about the students who do not push themselves in certain arenas because parents, teachers, peers, or society tell them they cannot do it. By high school, a lot of them have disengaged from the clubs, conversations, and classes that address bigger social issues. The little world they have constructed seems to be the only place where they feel they have power and know how things work. So I would rather be the teacher who is pushing too hard, who is encouraging them to take risks. You have to shake people out of their little boxes and then do something with that discomfort so they learn and grow.

MARGARET: One thing that has struck me is how terrified my kids are of taking risks and being wrong. There is a tremendous connection between the willingness to take a risk and the ability to learn anything, but I have to constantly reassure my students that who they are and what they know are okay. Do you all have to do that with your students?

PAUL: I don't.

JULIA: I do. Every year, I have students who want positive feedback at every step. By trying to make things accessible, we have created a culture of showing the students exactly what to do before asking them to do something exactly like it. My colleague calls this "show and go." But students need to risk doing something that is not totally structured, guided, and supported. We need to balance pushing kids to work through the stuff that is harder for them and giving them the tools they need to be successful in life. I have not figured out how to do this other than to explain to the students that when we do something new, they might get frustrated and make mistakes, so they need to be patient. But accepting potential failure is really hard for some kids.

MARGARET: So how did your kids feel about being in a study skills class, Julia?

JULIA: We talked about that at the beginning of the year. A lot of them said they were in the Reach Program because they were dumb, and that was hard. Apparently, some kids called our resource lab "the retard lab." I tried to talk to the kids about the different reasons they ended up in the class, which had nothing to do with intelligence. What I found most valuable was taking the students to tutor elementary school kids once a week. For example, Deondra, an African-American student with whom I had a particularly perplexing dynamic, was in her element and got a lot of really positive feedback when she was tutoring.

JOE: As we get harder and harder kids, I'm feeling now more than ever before that the parental role in my students' lives is the most crucial element in their development. If all a child knows is to respond by smacking someone across the back of the head, then …

MARGARET: Often at school, I feel like I can and should substitute for my students' mothers precisely because they can play out their parental conflicts with me in a more emotionally safe way. I recently became a stand-in parent for a student who has serious issues with her mom. She is devoted to me as a mother figure in all those nasty ways that only a thirteen-year-old girl can be. She never stops saying negative things to me, but she also never leaves me alone. She follows me around after school, goes into my desk, and, one day, wore my ID badge inside her shirt. I used to think that being a surrogate parent was not part of my job, but the older I get, the more I think that anything a child is and wants to do with me is part of my job.

JOE: I would agree with you and really respect you for taking that on, especially since many teachers these days feel they don't have time for that.

MARGARET: Sticking to the curriculum is definitely a safer place to be than letting a student chew me out in two languages before stealing my ID badge.

CONNIE: It seems like you're often a stand-in parent, too, Joe. Students are constantly asking you to help them in ways that extend well beyond your official school duties.

JOE: Maybe that's where I'm most valuable to them.

PAUL: Are there restrictions in what kind of relationships you can have with the kids, Joe?

JOE: There probably are rules in the district, but if a student asks me for a ride home or to take her to Planned Parenthood because she thinks she's pregnant, I'll do that. Maybe it will come back and nip me in the ass someday, but I'll take that on. I know my principal trusts that I've got the students' best interests at heart.

CONNIE: In your classroom, too, Paul, it seems like having students for three years allows you to develop really strong relationships with them. In contrast, you have noted, Margaret, that you feel well connected to your students just as it is time for them to leave your classroom.

JOE: The creation of community deserves more attention because community-building is such a powerful, powerful thing. I actively try to build community with my students and when it starts to happen, we examine why it is not really a desired part of a capitalist society. When you have community, you don't have to rely so much on buying stuff to make yourself feel whole.

JULIA: Or stepping on people to feel good.

JOE: Right. It doesn't feel good to be aggressive to other people in your community. But being part of a community is the most freeing thing you can possibly do with the rest of your life.

MARGARET: Have you been able to build that community with the tougher kids in your class, Joe?

JOE: If I'm lucky enough to have the seven kids in my class who need a lot of attention, and only those seven kids, for a stretch of time. It's not set up to happen on a regular basis, and, unfortunately, most staff members think that ninety-five percent of our population is not going to get what they need if we focus all of our attention on these particular kids. So we end up letting them go. I think that's a convenient answer, but it's the general consensus among the staff. I say give them to me, let me take them on the Appalachian Trail for six months, and I'll fix them. But who's going to fund that?

PAUL: Plenty of people feel that the only way to be effective with kids in more of a survival mode is to dress up in a suit, use certain language, and really keep them in line. You still make good positive connections with them and get to know their families and their local culture, but you are an authority figure who is never called by your first name.

MARGARET: This issue of using first names is interesting. I know that kids call you Joe and Paul at your schools, but this is the first year at my school where there has been a lot of variety in what children feel free to call me. I'm wondering if there's some kind of connection here between kids having more power in my classroom and trying out the breathtakingly exciting event of calling me Margaret to my face, in a classroom, in front of their classmates.

CONNIE: Margaret or Ms. Q-Tip.

JULIA: Ms. Q-tip? Someone called you Mrs. Q-tip!?

MARGARET: We did a research project on language, and Keith, who is a pretty hardcore kid, decided he was interested in slang. He came across a slang dictionary and saw the term *q-tip*, which apparently means a skinny old woman with white hair. I don't know that I'm skinny, but I certainly produce the gray hair, and he thought that was hilarious.

JULIA: That is hilarious!

MARGARET: I love it when kids call me *Ms. Q-tip* because it has become a term of endearment for a lot of the black kids and some of the white kids. A lot of the Spanish-speaking kids actually call me *vieja* (everyone starts laughing) but do it in a very sweet, respectful way. These different names for me have created an opportunity to talk about the process of naming, the language of respect, and the barriers that names can set up. Like one kid asked me, "How come you let Roberto call you Margaret, but you won't let Jamie do it?" I told him, "Because I like the way Roberto does it, and I don't like Jamie's tone of voice when she does it. You're allowed to pick what people call you, because that's about you." So we have been able to talk about when they can cross lines with names and when they are not welcome to do so.

JULIA: It does seem like your school, Margaret, provides an environment where kids can develop a genuine appreciation for learning and its rewards because their social and cultural identities are not at stake. It is hard to value the academic stuff if you don't feel accepted at school.

MARGARET: Yeah. Oftentimes, kids who are struggling in high school return to Johnson to get a fix. One of our former students recently came back and said, "I was such a jerk in middle school, but the teachers were so good to me here and cared about me so much." When he came back, we told him how wonderful he looked, how smart he is, and how we all knew he would do really well. He may or may not be doing that great, but he came back to hear some validation. It's like coming back to your family. Maybe Johnson does that for kids because we are part of the community and have a very stable teaching staff. It's a safe place for these kids, and maybe that is enough, along with whatever academics we can manage to work in. Maybe, for once, it's not a deficit that I'm white because that kid needs to hear that a white person thinks he's totally awesome exactly the way he is. I would like to think so because we all want to think we are doing something useful and valuable in the world, don't we?

PAUL: I think that kids probably trust you, like you to some extent, and see you as living a rich, happy life, Margaret. They can learn about a quality life from you because you are a solid, consistent part of theirs and are not giving up on them. You're also not doing your job because you have to but because it is interesting to you. It's not about being the cool or hip teacher either. The students see through that. It's about being sincere and vulnerable to some extent.

CONNIE: I've been in your classroom during many a lunch hour, Margaret, and cannot remember a single time when an eighth grader did not come by to visit you.

MARGARET: Yeah, they do. Our test scores, relative to the district, are always at the bottom, but I guess it is not always the academics that parents care about.

PAUL: Even at Lakeside, parents say they have to make a leap of faith about the academic part of what we do because they want a high quality of life for their kids. I just hope that the increasing impact of standardized tests does not disrupt the health of your school, Margaret, because right now it seems like a place that is safe for a diverse body of students to engage in schooling that builds a good attitude about the purpose of learning.

MARGARET: Well, it's certainly not perfect. For example, a young teacher sees me as encroaching on her turf with the Spanish-speaking students.

JOE: She wants to be the go-to teacher for those kids?

MARGARET: Yeah, and the kids like her. But she does not see that I can offer something of value by coming to them as a student of Spanish. We are not the same women to these students, and I feel vulnerable talking to her because she does not seem to recognize what a gift it has been to have these kids accept me into their community. I've worked really hard for my relationship with them. She doesn't understand that, and I don't know if that is because she is twenty-three years old or because she can no more understand who I am than I can understand who she is.

JOE: The truth of the matter is that it's a win-win for the students to have both of you there. I wonder if you also approach her as a student, might she be a little more open to you?

MARGARET: Well, I've spoken with her in Spanish, but she does not cut me any slack as a beginning speaker. It's almost like she's saying, "This is the way I speak Spanish. If you want to speak to me in Spanish, you can meet me where I live." I worry that she is going to polarize the Spanish-speaking population in the name of protecting them.

PAUL: I wonder though, Margaret, if there is an opportunity to collaborate with her at some level?

MARGARET: I offered her my perspective as someone who's been teaching these kids for sixteen years. She did not welcome it. Instead, she seemed resentful that I thought I knew anything, and I was angry that she thought I couldn't know anything because I am a white American woman.

PAUL: I would say that authority is probably involved in her resistance. I know when I've worked with different teaching partners that I have the privilege of seniority. You know, "I've done this longer than you." I try hard not to shut down conversations about possible classroom activities when my experience tells me how certain ideas are going to turn out.

JULIA: I think you have to treat her like she's one of your students, Margaret. There may be a time and place when she feels like you have something to offer her, but she's not there yet.

MARGARET: We've made enough peace to live with each other, and you're right, Julia. I've made the offer, and she will come to me if she decides to do so. I am hoping that the students' reactions to me will prove to her that I care a lot about these kids.

PAUL: There is so much competition between teachers, staff, and administration, but it's really important to have a classroom and school where there are strong, positive connections with everybody there. That is what Nel Noddings talks about—everything happens in moments when we are all present and trying to understand what's going on as best we can.[1] When we learn to be really good connectors in a community, that's a big success. How can we feel like what we are doing is social justice if we do it in isolation? It may be messy sometimes but—

JOE: It is messy when a student says, "I need you to help me get off heroin because I can't do it by myself." Aah, Jesus, you know!? You don't expect that, but when it's there, you have to deal with it. Luckily, I work in a school where the connections being made with our particular clientele are perceived as being far more important than the content we share with students. If you're keeping a kid from joining the gang scene or slitting his wrist tonight, well, gee, that's pretty valuable. Unfortunately, a relatively high percentage of the kids we work with are dealing with these issues.

One of my African-American students just got his second felony—possession of pot with intent to distribute. One more offense, and he goes to prison. And yesterday, I held a sweat lodge ceremony for a kid who is on the verge of committing suicide. It's been scary to see how much despair he is feeling. It's all about, "I don't want to die in a nuclear war," and, "We are destroying the planet." So I held a ceremony for him and a couple of his friends, hoping to give him another perspective. It's important to let these kids know there's an adult in the world who is an actual friend, not just an authority figure over them. That goes a long way toward their maturation. Whether or not that conforms to *No Child Left Behind,* I really don't care.

MARGARET: I would be so overwhelmed by the problems your students are facing, Joe. You cannot block out a kid who's shooting up or pregnant and say, "Well, okay, but we need to learn how to write a paragraph today."

PAUL: Yeah, I don't know about teaching life lessons to kids who are just surviving. I have kids who are just surviving, but not because of financial needs. Usually they are struggling with emotional issues, which is probably why they are at Lakeside instead of somewhere else.

MARGARET: That is just as immobilizing for a kid as anything else.

PAUL: But my students have a support network made up of people who know how to deal with the system and so can give them a leg up. And we intentionally try to develop that network in the classroom. In our art center this past week, we had kids represent a network of people who can help them stay safe and healthy—a protective behaviors network—by creating a hand.[2] The thumb represents their family, but the rest of the fingers represent four other adults to whom they can go when they need help. I emphasized to them that I can be one of those fingers but sometimes am going to be distracted and not able to listen to them effectively, so they need to keep going down the road until they find an adult who can help them.

CONNIE: The parallels between what the students and we want and need continually strike me. These protective networks are important for us, too.

PAUL: Well those connections are life. That's what it should be about, not a stupid multiple choice test that's going to label a kid, go into his file, and decide what his future is.

What Does It Mean to Care Critically?

Paul mentioned Nel Noddings at several of our monthly meetings, and her seminal work, *Caring: A Feminine Approach to Ethics and Moral Education,* undoubtedly relates to the notion of relational literacy. In 1984, Noddings wrote, "Caring involves stepping out of one's own personal frame of reference into the other's ... Our attention, our mental engrossment, is on the cared-for, not on ourselves. Our reasons for acting, then, have to do with the other's wants and desires and with the objective elements of his [or her] problematic situation" (24). Although teachers undoubtedly deserve to lead their own lives, apart from those of their students, and cannot alone resolve the macro-level injustices in which many of their students' lives are steeped (Anyon 2005), they often make a significant difference in their students' worlds. This is particularly so when they demonstrate authentic concern for their students' well-being.

In her ethnographic study of "at-risk, inner-city youth," Janelle Dance emphasizes a common characteristic of the students' favorite teachers: "the ability to convince students that they genuinely care" (2002, 75). Although I did not interview students in my study, I observed several caring behaviors in the four teachers' classrooms that included "[u]nderstanding and encouraging students, being someone whom students can talk and look up to, being concerned about students and having time for them" (Dance 2002, 75). As already noted in Julia's portrait, she helped students better understand lessons and complete assignments beyond class time. Such actions, which Margaret took on as well, corresponded to a caring that was tied to an "expectation of academic excellence" (Antrop-González and De Jesús 2006, 424). Julia and Margaret also demonstrated their concern for students by sharing food on a regular basis with those who were hungry. They did not ask students why they were hungry; Julia and Margaret just gave them food. I particularly remember one morning when a student came into Margaret's classroom before school started and quietly told Margaret she had not had breakfast. Margaret gave her food and discreetly said she could eat it in Margaret's desk cubby, away from the scrutiny of her peers. Paul also demonstrated an *"authentic* form of caring" that emphasized "relations of reciprocity between teachers and students" (Valenzuela 1999, 61, emphasis in original). He was constantly performing small but meaningful acts for the "cared-for," such as retrieving lip balm when he saw that one of his students' lips were badly chapped, attending his students' sporting events and musical performances, or bringing in resources for individual students that related to their interests, like a newspaper article on skateboarding.

Then there was Joe. The lengths he would go to keep his students alive and coming to school never ceased to amaze me. During the year I was in his classroom, Joe not only hosted the sweat lodge ceremony mentioned in the previous conversation, but he also invited students to his birthday party, frequently took students to nearby restaurants for lunch, and, during the fourth quarter, drove twenty-five extra miles each day to enable a student, who had moved out of town, to continue obtaining high school credits at Park.

Although these teachers' actions illustrate genuine caring, the problem remains that caring can render harmful as well as beneficial effects for students. Accordingly, elaborating the kinds of caring that contribute to a more just classroom, society, and world is necessary to legitimate my attention to relational literacy. Thankfully, Rene Antrop-González and Anthony De Jesús effectively reclaim *caring* with their theory of critical care, described as "the ways in which communities of color may care about and educate their own" that translate into "school cultures and practices aimed at engaging students in learning linked to broader goals of community survival and development" (2006, 413). In their study of two Puerto Rican and Latino schools, the students "explained that caring teachers offered them guidance and friendship inside and outside the classroom, held them to high academic expectations, and demonstrated a sense of solidarity by being active co-learners and facilitators rather than authoritarian teachers" (423).

In several critical respects, however, Antrop-González and De Jesús' (2006) theory of critical care does not apply to my study. Indeed, the educational setting in my research that most resembled the small, community-based schools in theirs was Paul's school, which parents organized and opened in 1972. This school, however, continues to align with their predominantly white, upper-middle-class values and interests rather than those of communities of color that are struggling to survive and develop. Additionally, the educational processes I observed in Margaret's classroom, and, to some extent, in Joe's and Julia's, as well, largely involved the teaching of "other people's children" (Delpit 1995) rather than teaching to protect one's own. Part of the conflict between Margaret and the new Spanish-speaking Latina teacher seemed related to this teacher's perception that Margaret was infringing on her territory by working so closely with *her* students.

Moreover, as noted in chapter four, Margaret was confronting some African-American students' accusations that she favored Latino students. My observations of Johnson Middle School and Margaret's depictions of events there—particularly the appearance of "English Only Table" signs at the school's Afro-Caribbean and Latino Celebration—indicated that the school was not confronting ethnic and racial divisions in the larger community. For the school culture to advance the "critical care" that Antrop-González and De Jesús (2006) promote, it would need to face a deep-seated black and brown conflict that, without intervention, will leave white supremacy unscathed.

Nevertheless, all of the teachers in this study exhibited characteristics of critical care. Although some of the language used during our group discussions suggested a deficit model of thinking (for example, striving to "fix" damaged children rather than to build on "students' cultural and linguistic knowledge and heritage" [Valenzuela 1999, 25]), their spoken words belied the authentically caring teacher-student relationships I observed in all four classrooms. When I refer to relational literacy, then, I am denoting processes that develop teacher-student relationships centered on mutual trust, respect, and responsibility sharing. These processes not only create positive dyadic relationships between the teacher and individual students but also advance a classroom and, ideally, school-wide community in which relational reciprocity is honored and every individual's dignity is protected. Significantly, relational literacy is largely modeled rather than explicitly taught. Students see and feel teachers treating them with respect and, in turn, leave their classrooms with a paradigm of compassionate human relationships.

Notably, the breaking down of hierarchical relationships between teachers and students, a key aspect of relational literacy, was more prominent in the less-traditional classrooms. Although all of the teachers were "willing to be learners with their students," Joe and Paul could more easily assume the roles of "active co-learners and facilitators" than Julia and Margaret (Antrop-González and De Jesús 2006, 422, 423). As highlighted in the previous conversation, Joe and Paul encouraged their students to call them by their first names, a practice endorsed and followed by their larger school communities. Intentionally addressing community members by their first names helped to equalize teacher-student relationships and stressed mutual understanding more than social control. This practice also enabled Joe to realize his stated goal of offering students a genuine adult friendship that was "respectful and evocative of student development" (Antrop-González and De Jesús 2006, 422). Nevertheless, the message that teachers and students are relative equals can and did cause problems in Paul's classroom, where many of the students had a well-established sense of entitlement. I elaborate on this issue in the next chapter but want to note here that promoting mutual respect does not translate into children taking for granted the wisdom that commonly accompanies more years lived on this earth.

A facet of critical care that Joe did not abide was the maintenance of strong teacher-student boundaries (Antrop-González and De Jesús 2006, 422), which, as I described in his portrait, sometimes landed him in hot water. Nevertheless, he understood his students' daily realities to such an extent that they held him in extremely high regard, as evidenced by a note that one of his students, Michelle, gave him on "Teacher Appreciation Day." Michelle described being "lost in who she was" until accompanying Joe to the Sun Dance ceremony, adding, "I cannot thank you enough." Although Joe struggled to engage some of his African-American students, he consistently saw himself and "the destiny of humanity" in all of his students, thereby treating each "as worthy beneficiaries of [his] wisdom, information, trust, and caring" (Dance 2002, 84). Joe was fully present to the students, and they responded in kind (Noddings 1984).

Conclusion

In closing this chapter on relational literacy, I want to emphasize a "process theory of caring," as it "provides insight to the potential complexities and contradictions inherent within caring interactions, interpretations, expressions, and contexts" (McKamey, in Antrop-González and De Jesús 2006, 413). The "close, high-quality interpersonal relationships" (Antrop-González and De Jesús 2006, 422) that all of the teachers developed with their students were not unflawed but were continuously strived for, an effort that merits significant attention and appreciation in a discussion on education for social justice. Moreover, these relations toward the *cared-for*, even if they were sometimes exhausting and painful, sustained the teachers in their work. To use Noddings's eloquent words, because our "very individuality is defined in a set of relations," we are not naturally alone but, rather, are naturally in relation with others from whom we "derive nourishment and guidance" (1984, 51).

Regrettably, part of the relational complexities and contradictions within caring involve linguistic misunderstandings and faulty assumptions about groups of people, which burden our interactions with individual members of those groups. These relational missteps, whether intentional or unconscious, influence judgments, feelings, and behavior, which in turn shape policy decisions (Wilson 2002). Consequently, even an education that develops critically enlightened and caring citizens does not always realize vibrant, just democratic communities. We also need communication skills that allow us to expose and address conflict and controversial issues nonviolently. Indeed, one of the best ways to deduce the "nature of our hidden minds"—and surface our unfounded biases—is through interaction with others (Wilson 2002, 16). To support these claims, I turn to Paul's classroom and the noteworthy democratic literacy cultivated within it.

PART IV

DEMOCRATIC LITERACY

7

Democratic Literacy in Context

A Portrait of Paul

"Okay folks, time for dates in history," Paul said. A man of medium build, he wore his brown, shoulder-length hair in a neat ponytail. Paul's twinkling eyes made a mystery of his age. It was a cold February morning, and the students had just returned from their differentiated math classes—the only subject area for which Paul's students were separated into sixth, seventh, and eighth grades. The students formed a circle as they sat down for the morning meeting, which took place every day and lasted thirty to forty-five minutes.

"The first date is February 21, 1804, when British engineer Richard Trevithick demonstrated the first steam engine ever to run on rails," Paul said. "What do you all know about the industrial revolution?"

A student shot her hand up in the air and waved it frantically.

"Laura, what would you like to say?" Paul asked as he made eye contact with the bespectacled brunette student. Laura was completing her final year at Lakeside, or eighth grade in a traditional school. She had been in Paul's classroom for two and a half years and at Lakeside since kindergarten.

"England started to replace wood with coal because it burned better and the country had lots of it," Laura responded matter-of-factly. "Coal let England expand its steel industry, but people had to keep digging deeper and deeper mines to get at the coal. So the first steam engine was actually made to pump water out of these mines."

"Thank you, Laura. Amy, did you have something to add?" Paul asked, nodding at a lanky girl, who often seemed too mature for her thirteen-year-old body.

"Factories used a lot of child labor," Amy gushed. "These kids worked really long hours and were often abused by their bosses. I saw pictures of kids who were like nine years old and filthy from the factory. It was really sad."

"Thank you, Amy. Last comment about this date in history from Brandon," Paul said and pointed to a freckle-nosed student sitting on a stool, patiently holding up his hand.

"The mining camps created upper and lower classes," Brandon stated, "because the owners got richer and richer off the mine's profits. Most of the workers' wages went back to the owners because they charged the workers to live in their," Brandon made quotation marks with his fingers, "company towns."

"Many of you know a lot about the industrial revolution," Paul affirmed, "and have already studied it, or aspects of it, in here." He briefly summarized how capitalism and technological advances propelled the creation of factories and railroads before saying, "Alright, let's move on to the second date in history." Paul proceeded to discuss the life of English poet W. H. Auden, who was born on February 21, 1907. He read aloud "Musee des Beaux-Arts," a poem about human apathy for other people's suffering, and explained Auden's reference to a Brueghel painting.

Paul glanced at the clock and quickly moved on to the third and final date. "On February 21, 1939, the 'high priestess of soul,' Nina Simone, was born," he said. "I'm going to play you the song 'To Be Young, Gifted, and Black,' which she first performed in 1969." After telling the students a little more about Simone's life and the history of the song, he placed her album on the record player and laid down the needle. The students listened intently to the lyrics. When the song was over, Paul asked, "What do you make of that?"

Becky, a second-year student with a zany sense of humor and bohemian flare for fashion, spoke first. "It's good that they're proud and all, but why do they have to be young and black?"

"What bugs you about that, Becky?" Paul asked. After several seconds of silence, he said gently, "Do you want to leave it at that for now?"

She nodded, and Paul called on Ashley, an articulate "eighth grader" with short red hair.

"Well, people were young and gifted, but doors were closed to them at that time, because they were black," Ashley replied.

Mindy spoke next. "Nina Simone was trying to counteract all the people who had locked out black people," she said, furrowing her brow and resting her chin on her hand.

"But there's this emphasis on black," Becky insisted. "What about other colors?"

Paul responded, "Let's think about the intended audience of this song and how people gain self-worth when they are oppressed. Think about gay rights today or women during the civil rights movement. Think about how people develop confidence."

Becky replied defensively, "I didn't mean that ..."

"I'm just suggesting that we think about how change comes about," Paul emphasized.

With an air of authority, Brad, another student in his second year, said, "We need to remember that this song was written around the time that Martin Luther King Jr. was shot, the black power salute was given at the Olympics, and the Vietnam War was happening."

"I think the song was trying to encourage those who couldn't get into college to keep going, to keep pushing," Brandon added.

"It's an optimistic message," Paul agreed. "There's a lot more to be said about this, but we need to move on."

A Brief History of Paul

Setting the Scene: On a late December morning, Connie has come to Lakeside School to interview Paul in his classroom. She is meeting him for the first time after a university colleague recommended that she recruit him for her study. Connie gave Paul a list of tentative interview questions, and he is addressing the first one by describing his family background and how he came to be a teacher.

I'm from this state and grew up in a big family. My family has a lot to do with who I am. My dad was a high school biology teacher, and my mom raised the family but was also politically active. Both of my parents were active, but my mom led the way with her concern about our society and governance. She always looked out for the underdog and involved us in community organizations and events when we were kids. I remember going to retirement homes and my siblings raising money for food pantries.

I grew up on a small hobby farm, which also influenced my teaching and work ethic. My parents raised us very frugally, and I remember openly critical conversations about snobby attitudes. The farm was located near a really white small town, but when I was young, my family would go to the city of Raintree quite a bit. My mom worked in a summer day camp there for what they called the Congress of Racial Equality—the CORE. We would go to a Catholic church in Raintree, where the priest was a civil rights activist, and march for open housing. We were just one big white family marching along with the mostly African-American community there.

I did my undergraduate education at the university here and ended up triple majoring in philosophy, political science, and economics. When I graduated, I didn't know what I was going to do professionally, but my longtime partner was living in Rhode Island, so I decided to move there. I worked as a teaching assistant in this home for boys that had a small school attached to it. They were wards of the state—ages five to fourteen—and a very sad, rough bunch. During that time, I also went to the van Gogh museum in Amsterdam. I love his work, which is very moving but also very sad. When I came out of the museum, there were children playing in a park area. I thought to myself, kids are therapeutic. (Paul laughs.) So through the combination of my Amsterdam epiphany, working in this school for boys, and my mom and sister's encouragement to become a teacher, I decided to come back and enroll in the special education program. I chose it because I wanted to work with the populations that struggle to have a go at our society.

But I wasn't really happy with the courses I took. I didn't like the behaviorist viewpoint promoted in the special ed department. Then, there was this moment when I went to a professor and said I was interested in androgyny and gender issues. His response to my topic of research was, 'Oh, that's a waste of time. It's meaningless.' Frustrated with the field of psychology, I decided to get a regular teaching degree and so was certified in first through eighth grades. During that time, I also worked in day care, which influenced my interest in theme-based centers. In a lot of cases, integrating the arts, movement, music, and all the disciplines under a theme makes for a really rich learning environment. It also makes a lot of sense, which I understood from my overlapping college majors.

I did my student teaching in a combined first- and second-grade class. My cooperating teacher helped me learn the skills to map out an integrated curriculum. The kids would facilitate the morning group times, and that was really impressive to me. The teacher would be in the room but sometimes wouldn't even be sitting with the group. I learned an awful lot from her, especially about multiage grouping and how that is very natural at whatever age. So when I ended up at Lakeside, I felt comfortable and ethical. *Ethical* is a descriptor I use for working here. I think it's a very moral way to learn, teach, and live.

But before I took a job here, I went to Boston for two years. Because my certification didn't transfer, and since it felt like we were only going to be there a little while, I took a long-term sub position in a Boston middle school. The student diversity was spectacular to me—whites were the minority, many students were from lower-income homes, and a lot of kids were bused in from Roxbury. The largest population was African-American, but there were also Asian and Latino families there. I remember there being a bilingual program that was separated from the rest of the school because of Title I. One classroom in the school was run a little like Lakeside by this older teacher, a white man who had a lot of experience. The Chinese-American principal said to him, 'Okay, you take the troubled kids. Just make sure they stay out of our hair.' So this guy ran an open classroom. I spent some time in there and was impressed with what he was doing with these middle schoolers. I ended up liking that age and had two years of experience at the middle school level when I came back.

Upon my return, I found out that my teaching file with the district wasn't open for some reason. At that time, a friend, who is also an educator, had kids at Lakeside. She said, 'I think you'd fit at Lakeside.' So I applied here and got the job. I've been here ever since. Eighteen years. For a long time I would say, 'Wellll, I may move. I may go to the public school system.' It's a real tension for me that I work in a private school. My parents are strong supporters of public education, and so am I. It was hard for my dad, a teacher and union representative, to tell people that I taught in a private school. It's still hard. I think it sounds odd to a lot of people that I'm a supporter of public education when I'm a teacher in a private school.

Paul and Karen's Classroom

The classroom in which Paul and Karen, his co-teacher, worked held many learning objects. A variety of musical instruments, including a guitar, clarinet, flute, and zither, rested atop a wooden cabinet by the door. Assorted artifacts lined a high shelf on the front wall holding the chalkboard. Each relic—a metal cheese grater, empty Reddi Whip can, old Lemon Drop metal box, broken alarm clock, Barbie doll—had its own story. A low-lying table in front of the chalkboard was a repository for the current newspaper and books in use, like *Herstory: Women Who Changed the World* and Walter Dean Myer's *Fallen Angels,* a novel that Paul and Karen were reading aloud to the students about an African-American teenager in Harlem who becomes a soldier in the Vietnam War.[1] On a nearby bookshelf was a record player, surrounded by the LPs that Paul played during morning meetings, such as Janis Joplin's *Pearl* and Dolly Parton's *Coat of Many Colors.* He often used music to discuss social issues. Beside the blackboard stood an easel with a voluntary, daily learning challenge posted on it. For example, one challenge was to re-create part of van Gogh's *Starry Night* from a color reprint.

A bulletin board covering the north wall held the Universal Declaration of Human Rights; news clippings, such as articles about a recent neo-Nazi rally and the anniversary of school desegregation in Little Rock, Arkansas; information related to the class's current curriculum, such as a Cirque du Soleil pamphlet for the circus unit or information about embryonic stem cell research for the diversity and genetics unit; and a gay pride alliance statement. The counter below the bulletin board might house microscopes one week and fruit flies the next, depending on the thematic unit under study. On the south side of the room, five computers occupied the space below a carpeted loft with oversized pillows, where students could read and study. A bookshelf filled with young adult novels, nonfiction books, atlases, and a host of other reading materials stood behind the computers.

At the beginning of each year, Paul and Karen allowed the students to negotiate the location and formation of their desk clusters. In September 2005, some students opted to line up several desks along the east wall, where large windows overlooked the school's sloping front lawn; two others connected their desks in the room's center. Paul and Karen also encouraged students to personalize the wooden boards attached to their desks. The resulting color combinations and designs contributed to the already vibrant atmosphere of the room.

Thematic learning stations appeared throughout the classroom. For each unit, there were social studies, science, literacy, and art centers. Each center included written instructions, student handouts, and additional learning materials. For example, the art center during the genetics and diversity unit held clay of multiple colors. Every student blended the clay until it matched his or her skin tone. Paul and Karen then displayed these different hues, as well as the students' one-word characterization of their skin colors, at the front of the room.

In their classroom, Paul and Karen acted as facilitators of knowledge construction, not experts or authority figures. To reinforce this role, they emphasized the need for interpretation in addition to fact-finding, pointed out their lack of knowledge on particular subjects, and publicly acknowledged mistakes when they made them. Although they used direct, whole-class instruction at times, such as when they taught a weekly workshop on writing, most of their work involved creating learning activities and then guiding that learning as it took place. Accordingly, the students had a lot of unstructured work time to complete both learning center activities and long-term projects, such as an independent research proposal, presentation, and paper.

The students also engaged in a variety of activities outside room 202, some of which were taught by other teachers or involved students from other classrooms. For example, the students met twice a week for Spanish instruction and weekly for art, music, "creative inspirations" ("short activities desired to inspire the imagination"), literature circles, and "book partners" (where older students were paired with younger students from other classrooms for oral reading and book discussions). Additionally, they visited the library every week to participate in "technology integration projects" and learn about new young adult literature. Once a month, the students also joined the rest of the school for "Friday Follies," which included student and staff performances of various kinds.

Additionally, Lakeside students had access to various learning opportunities that outside resource people brought into the school. For example, one parent, who was an English professor at the university, led an optional literature group on Charles Dickens's work. Some university students majoring in music also offered Lakeside students African drumming, guitar, marimba, and stomp classes. Guest speakers and performance troupes frequently visited the school, and the students were encouraged to take their talents out into the community, as well. After the students completed the circus unit, for instance, Lakeside not only held a school-wide circus, complete with a ringmaster, band, stilt-walking, and student-made puppet show, but Lakeside staff also encouraged students to perform their acts in a citywide youth circus. Furthermore, Paul facilitated a "Kids Night Out" theater, for which students wrote scripts, created stages, and performed skits before a live audience.

The students in Paul and Karen's classroom also had frequent opportunities to shape the curriculum. During the weeklong student-led unit, for example, the students chose to follow Karen and Paul's instructional model by creating various subject area centers on topics like cat and dog behavior, the cultures and histories of Asian countries, rocket propulsion (students used baking soda and vinegar to launch their handmade paper and plastic rockets), home design, and capitalism (via a simulation called "eggonomics"). A controversial ritualistic worshipping of one student also occurred during this unit, resulting in a phone call from a concerned parent. Overall, however, the students enjoyed taking responsibility for their own learning and came up with innovative strategies to teach and learn engaging content. Moreover, Paul, Karen, and the student teacher enjoyed being students for a week. As Paul wrote in an evaluation handout about the student-led unit,

> Karen and I know that it is important for people your age to learn the skills to be positive members of any community that you are a part of—now and in the future ... Part of a democratic society is sharing power and knowing that we can learn from each other. I experienced both of those things and found it educationally valuable, exciting and stimulating.

The students also participated significantly in the evaluation of their own learning. Each week, they filled out a "check-in" sheet, which they went over with Paul or Karen in one-on-one conferences at the end of the week. Additionally, they created a student portfolio for each unit, which Karen and Paul showed to parents during parent-teacher conferences. The portfolio displayed the skills and content knowledge students had learned, their progress toward social and academic goals, and reflections on their progress "as a student and as a person." More specifically, students included three types of work from each unit in their portfolios: an ordinary piece that represented a basic level of understanding about and response to a topic, an extraordinary piece that represented a student's "increased confidence in learning and high quality response (product) to an activity," and a growth piece that represented an area of learning upon which the student needed to improve. Rather than issuing grades, then, Paul and Karen assessed student learning through student portfolios, students' written self-evaluations, and individual conversations with the students. Additionally, in lieu of a report card, Paul and Karen wrote lengthy narratives about each student's academic and social progress.

The school's website offered an apt summary of the "progressive education" that took place in Paul and Karen's classroom:

> "Progressive education" is about creating an environment in which children's strengths and unique ways of learning are supported. We teach children to be in charge of their learning—to be thinkers, challengers, and wonderers.
>
> We don't teach for the test. We teach to learn. We teach understanding the concepts behind the facts. At Lakeside, asking, "How did you get the answer?" is just as important as the answer itself.

About Lakeside School

"I learned a lot from the kids when I first came to Lakeside," Paul said roughly thirty minutes into the interview. "They helped me through the first part of my teaching here, which is part of Lakeside's philosophy—the kids have a big hand in what the curriculum is, how the classroom runs, and what the classroom culture is like. I sometimes use the label *democratic education* to describe the activities of the senior class.

"I don't have a master's degree," Paul continued, "but I've taken course work and done action research that I presented at the American Educational Research Association conference." He laughed, a sign of his ever-present humility. "I'm involved in a research project right now about the roles that sound plays in learning."

"How many students do you have in here?"

"Twenty-four."

"And you have a co-teacher?"

"Yeah, Karen. To be honest, I wouldn't want to teach in isolation anymore. I've become a better person, teacher, and professional by working in collective groups."

"So how would you describe Lakeside as an educational institution?" I asked.

"According to the jargon, it's a progressive school. It includes more student involvement in developing curriculum and multiage, team-based teaching and learning. We don't test or grade the kids, and we try to build on internal rather than external motivation for learning. The school draws on humanistic psychology, like the work of Carl Rogers.

"It's not a free school though," Paul continued. "There's structure, and there are times of day when we insist that kids participate in learning activities."

"Since Lakeside is a private school, what sort of financial assistance or other kinds of aid is there?" I asked.

"There is some scholarship," Paul replied, "but I don't think anyone feels it is what it should be. There's this balance between the retention of teachers and the economic diversity of the student population, since eighty percent of tuition goes toward teacher and staff salaries. As with everywhere, our benefits and salaries cost more, although they are still eighty percent of public school teachers'. To maintain staff retention, the tuition has gone up. But some families will sacrifice quite a bit to send their kids here because they believe in the philosophy."

"If you don't mind my asking, what is the annual cost of tuition at Lakeside?"

"Oh, boy. It's about ten thousand two hundred dollars now. It's expensive."

"Do you have admission criteria?"

"We don't test kids for admission. However, the building is not accessible, and we don't have anyone licensed in special ed here. So there are some individuals and families we can't service because either the facility is not accommodating or we don't have the necessary skills. A lot of kids who end up here have labels attached to them, but we try not to use those labels. We even try not to use grade-level labels. I mean if you ask kids what grades they're in, they'll tell you. But we know how powerful language is and labels can be. We end up with quite a few kids who are labeled as having Asperger's syndrome. It's not that we shy away from learning about the research and strategies for helping kids like that learn; we just try not to use the labels."

"So, right back to the labels," I said, laughing, "how would you describe the demographics of the student population?"

"We have a large Jewish population. I think right now a quarter of my students—five or six—are practicing Jews. Then, because of the university, there's some ethnic diversity, but this city's not very ethnically diverse. We have a couple of kids who would probably identify as African-American, one as Thai-American, one as Filipino-Pakistani-American, and one as Indian-American. The rest would be Euro-Americans of various blends.

"There have been school committees that wanted to investigate the history of ethnic diversity at Lakeside. It's still a mystery why there isn't more diversity here, especially from the African-American community. One of the theories is that we lack African-American teachers. We have one teacher who would self-identify as African-American, and she's the first black teacher since I've been here. There's also the issue of whether progressive, open classrooms effectively serve kids of color in our society. That is an interesting issue, but I think progressive, democratic education offers a way for kids to understand the systems that they're going to encounter and learn strategies for helping to change or navigate those systems successfully. Most of the kids leave here and go into more traditional-looking settings for high school, so we try to teach them the skills they will need to do well in those places—like how to get good grades—but in a critical way."

"So you're trying to make explicit to them the rules of the game?" I asked.

"Yeah, and we talk about it that way and try to get them to think about what motivates them to learn. Many of them learn because they want to learn, which high school teachers love. Because these students have not been pounded down by the idea that grades are the only thing that matters, they don't say, 'What do we need to know for the test?'

"It is frustrating though," Paul said, sighing, "because a lot of the families here are fairly wealthy and have a lot of cultural capital. For those kids who don't have as much as others, there is cultural conflict in and outside of school. For example, there are different attitudes about material things and doing activities that cost a lot of money, like skiing or even going to the movies. I try to find inexpensive ways to give kids experiences, such as camping at a state park, visiting museums, and ice-skating on a nearby lake. We also teach the kids how to ride the bus and go on urban adventures—go out and about in the community and see what stuff is going on around here. But I think issues about money really should be more openly discussed.

"Actually, about twelve years ago, there was a real effort among the staff and members of the board, too, to base tuition on a sliding scale. Basically, parents would pay what they could afford. But some families went ballistic at the idea. Sometimes, I'm shocked to see how conservative a lot of these self-proclaimed liberal lefties are. Some even meddle in the classroom and how it functions. There's this entitlement with a private school: 'I have the money to come here, and I pay for your salary, Bub.'

"That kind of thing happens in public schools, too," Paul continued, "but I think it's more pronounced here. I don't know how much the greater Lakeside community, the families and parents, are really invested in seeing this school as an institution for social change, for social reconstruction. We added that to our descriptor, by the way, that we have a social reconstructionist curriculum. I actually only know what goes on in my classroom, and I question whether I can use the label *social justice educator* to describe myself. Certainly that language and *democratic education* are thrown around. But since it's a private school that is not funded by the tax system, it's hard for me to call it a democratic school. There are restrictions about coming here because of the tuition."

"One thing I wanted to ask you about, which you just alluded to, is how parental involvement plays out at Lakeside—how parents are interacting with you about their kids."

"Well, I think a good, healthy democracy involves conflict," Paul replied. "I try not to shy away from conflict. That is to say that I learn a lot from other staff members, students, and parents. But we certainly butt heads sometimes. We're reading a book by Avi about a teacher-student conflict that ultimately gets a teacher fired.[2] It's appropriate and ironic because while reading it, out of the corner of my eye, I'm watching two kids who have been going home and reporting stuff about me to their parents, kind of like what this kid in the book did. They're not taking responsibility for their own bad behavior," Paul said, laughing.

"That's part of teaching here," Paul continued, "because it's more informal. We don't have a huge set of rules for the kids and negotiate a lot of stuff. We want kids to question and know why we do certain things. In a lot of ways, the environment is more emotionally rich and charged for the kids and staff. But sometimes I feel it's more dangerous."

"Do you feel like the parents have trust in you as the *authority*?" I paused. "I hate to use that word in a school striving for more democratic relations."

"Well, I'm thinking of democratic education in terms of teaching students skills to participate in our democracy. They don't have full rights as citizens yet, and that's very important. Parents also don't have full rights to tell me what to do as a professional. They can try to do that, but that doesn't mean I'm going to do what they say."

"How's the support from your director when it comes to parental pressures?"

"She's really good about negotiating family cultures and what goes on in the school. So if there's a family who thinks that good handwriting is really important, we try to improve their kid's handwriting. To some degree, we want to support what families find valuable and important. But then there are times that we don't agree. Sometimes, you have to take away some individual liberties for the benefit of the whole group. That doesn't sit well with some kids or parents. Some kids want a more traditional classroom with textbooks, grades, and testing. But this sort of modification is contrary to parts of our mission and philosophy. So you have to look at the school's constitution and the teachers who are here and ask if they are willing to run the classroom differently for those individuals. I think all of this negotiation is healthy, but sometimes it's really exhausting.

"I just try to be really fair about it," Paul said. "When I first started here, I was much more rigid about protecting my professional integrity. I didn't think I should modify things just because families or kids disagreed with me. I still think the label *professional* is important; we need to be recognized and taken seriously as professionals who have a difficult job. But now I'm more flexible and sometimes wonder if I go too far," Paul said.

"I have to be careful about negotiating with other staff members," he continued, "because we want to be seen as a whole community—a team that communicates openly—not as individuals making decisions that don't involve the rest of the group. Like I said, a core part of democracy is deliberation, and the school should model that."

"It sounds like your director is on board with you all having a horizontal, democratic structure within the school," I said.

"Yeah, pretty much. She came out of retirement to take the position as Lakeside director in large part because she sees the potential of institutions as forces for social change."

"Did the teachers have a say in her hiring?"

"Oh, yeah," Paul replied, "and the students did, too. I'm very happy she's here. She's a promoter of having the staff do more professional development around multicultural education and is working to have greater diversity here."

"You've talked about the philosophy here, but is there a central mission statement that everyone needs to get on board with to be hired?"

"There needs to be familiarity with what progressive education is and what it means to create curriculum with kids as well as have respect for the potential of children. Is there a thing that we could all chant and be in agreement about?" We both laughed.

"There used to be something called the Lakeside Way," Paul said, "which no one really defined clearly. I know we would all be in agreement with some statements, but we definitely differ about how to implement and define responsibility. I like to bring up Vivian Paley's idea of 'You can't say you can't play.'[3] Our staff has a good discussion about that issue, and we're able to see where we stand. Setting the limits for recess is another place where differing ideas of responsibility come out. I sit on a recess committee with two students from the other senior classroom, and we're collecting quantitative data for a participatory action research project."

"That's fantastic," I said. "Well, would you describe the staff as fairly tight-knit community despite the frictions you've just mentioned?"

"That goes up and down over the years. In terms of just getting along with each other, though, we're doing really well. So I think now would actually be a good time to raise some issues. I think it's Nel Noddings who talks about building connections as the fundamental element of what education should be.[4] We've built connections among the staff, and so now we can push a little harder and challenge each other more.

"On the other hand, I don't know how teaching here compares to other settings, but any teaching situation is awfully demanding if you do it well. It's hard to do extra stuff. My partner has said that our teaching is the political stuff that we do and that it's probably enough. But, personally," Paul laughed, "I don't think it's enough for me."

A Tension Between Critical Thinking and Entitlement

"Why do all the cool people have to die?"
—*Lakeside student, upon hearing of Coretta Scott King's death*

As I became more familiar with Paul's classroom, I felt increasingly conflicted about what I observed there. On the one hand, Paul and Karen regularly created inspired learning opportunities and offered thoughtful guidance to the students, motivating their learning and helping them think critically about the subject matter at hand, as well as knowledge more generally. On the other hand, the critical lessons that the students learned, about poverty and racism, for example, seemed to give the students more discursive tools to add to their already impressive stash of cultural capital. In many ways, the students seemed to be learning the language of social justice but not necessarily understanding the suffering that accompanies economic and cultural injustices or the relinquishing of privileges that accompanies the redistribution of power and wealth.

Paul effectively raised critical consciousness at every turn and, consequently, his students understood that Coretta Scott King's political activism merited celebration. But I was not sure they understood on more than a superficial and rational level what she had been fighting for, or against. I also worried that they, like some of their parents, might use critical literacy to legitimate their elite positions in a social order that sustains itself via unjust economic and cultural processes. In other words, teaching students the rules of a social system that already benefits them could have the unintentional effect of strengthening that very system.

Annette Lareau's (2003) ethnography on children and the U.S. class system helped me theorize the uneasiness I often felt in Paul's classroom. Lareau describes middle-class parents as engaging in a process of "concerted cultivation" to ensure that their children maximally realize their individual talents. Part of this cultivation includes the parents' organization of numerous adult-led activities for their children, such as soccer, piano lessons, and ballet. Additionally, parents adhere to guidelines issued by professionals, including but not limited to teachers, doctors, and counselors. These guidelines "typically stress the importance of reasoning with children and teaching them to solve problems through negotiation rather than with physical force" (4). As a result of concerted cultivation strategies, "a robust sense of entitlement takes root in the children. This sense of entitlement plays an especially important role in institutional settings, where middle-class children learn to question adults and address them as relative equals" (2).

Regarding the latter point, students frequently challenged Paul's authority in the classroom in ways that I found disrespectful. One example of students assuming a sense of relative equality with Paul occurred during a conversation about an algebra course that students could take at the high school as Lakeside "seniors." A number of students openly dismissed Paul's claims, based on years of experience with this high school class, about its potential drawbacks. More specifically, Paul emphasized that students should consult their Lakeside teachers, who knew their academic strengths and weaknesses, before enrolling in the course because the high school wanted some assurance that they would succeed. One student responded, "It's a lot less scary than Paul's making it sound." Even after Paul clarified that some students had had a terrible experience with the course, this same student added, "This is not a big deal. I think everyone should do it."

Numerous times, I also remarked in my field notes that many of Paul's students saw privileges as entitlements. During a conversation with two students in which I asked about their "pogo-ball" performance for the circus, for instance, Laura snidely remarked that Lakeside didn't "have enough money for pogo sticks" and so had to settle for the inferior pogo-ball. This comment reminded me of the middle-class fourth-grader in Lareau's study, Garrett Tallinger, who was bothered by the insufficient wealth of his family, which prevented him from returning to private school. As Lareau wrote, "He takes for granted the fact that his parents can afford the cost of clothing, groceries, fast food, cars, medical appointments, and assorted activities for their children … He can't—and doesn't—even imagine that for working-class and poor children, these same taken-for-granted items and opportunities are viewed as (unavailable) *privileges*" (2003, 60, emphasis in original). Through no fault of their own, many students in Paul's class, like Laura, took for granted the many advantages they had in their daily lives and at Lakeside, not the least of which was the school's ability to put on an impressive circus. The air they breathed included travels to Europe, private guitar lessons, participation in an Israeli folk dancing group, organized club basketball, and membership in the city's youth choir.

Nevertheless, I want to reiterate that Paul and Karen worked hard to make the students' privileges visible to them through critical curricular lessons and experiences. For example, they used *Teaching Tolerance* materials, like *Us and Them,* as well as guest speakers to learn about various forms of oppression; exposed their students to Augusto Boal's *Theatre of the Oppressed*; and took students to a Rennie Harris Puremovement performance, which used hip-hop dance theater to address social issues like racism.[5] These lessons contributed to some students openly acknowledging that their advantages were privileges rather than entitlements. During one recess period, for instance, I overheard Paul tell a couple of students not to bring their iPods out of the classroom because they were not supposed to have them in the rest of the school. As part of his research on sound, Paul was temporarily allowing students to bring in such devices if students felt they improved their learning. After observing this interaction between Paul and the two students, another student, Ashley, commented that because some students couldn't afford iPods, they might feel uncomfortable when other students used them in the classroom.

Her peer Brent responded, "We're at Lakeside. Of course they can afford iPods."

Ashley retorted, "Have you ever heard of scholarships?"

At this point, Karen, Paul's co-teacher, intervened by emphasizing that some parents had made great sacrifices to send their kids to Lakeside.

Ashley saw this as an opportunity to rub in her victory. "Yeah, right. So they can't buy them iPods."

Karen then suggested that Ashley sign up to lead a morning meeting discussion on the issue of bringing iPods into the classroom. If Ashley ended up leading this discussion, I do not doubt that the class had a lively discussion about the iPod issue or that they negotiated a resolution with which everyone could live. The numerous opportunities that students had in Paul and Karen's classroom to collaborate successfully with their peers and adults allowed them to develop valuable social skills that will benefit their interpersonal relationships for years to come.

Perhaps the students in Paul's classroom will use their critical knowledge and negotiation skills to fight for economic redistribution and an end to cultural imperialism. Their repeated performance of entitled selves, however, suggests that they might also use these skills to make "bureaucratic institutions work to their advantage" and "accommodate their individual needs," regardless of or without attention to how such actions impact those less fortunate than themselves (Lareau 2003, 245).

Paul's Philosophy of Teaching

"Do you think you would be able to make a nutshell statement about your philosophy of teaching?" I asked toward the end of my interview with Paul.

Paul laughed in reply. "To me it's so complicated." He paused. "My partner has come up with a phrase, *artful science,* and I think that's a nice description of what teaching for anybody really is.

"Being in a small K–8 school, I see what a great thing it is for kids of different ages to mix, and for teachers of various ages to mix, too. Having the kids for three years, they really get to know me, and I get to know them and their families. I've seen some of them grow up because if they had older siblings who were already students here, I knew them when they were three or four years old. This experience builds on the idea of being receptive to what people are capable of doing but also recognizing what, developmentally speaking, they're not able to do.

"I often think of young adolescents' experience in this society as a sort of pretend TV version of young adulthood, where they're trying to act like what they think adults should act like. It gets very sick and twisted. Here, they can still be playful and kid-like, but they can also take on a lot of responsibility and behave very maturely.

"I think our educational system often tries to do what we do with our national pastimes, with our sports. In football, for instance, you have these measurements and lines on the field. It's all gridded out and is supposed to be very scientific, when the fact is, these guys are just going at each other. It's the guise of structure that's there in the gridiron and all that crap. But if you're supposed to be so scientific and all, where's the grace, beauty, and uniqueness out on the field? I think our culture often treats education as if it can be all mapped out with statistics and beeyugh." Paul scrunched his mouth as if he were swallowing a bitter pill.

"There's actually some beauty in the human error of the players and referees out on the field. Improvisation and creative, different styles of play are all parts of a beautiful game. It's a different," Paul paused. "I can't believe I'm using sports metaphors! If the military language starts slipping in, just kick me. Anyway, being in a group that has a collective nature—that builds trust and allows us to support each other in our work and learning—that in and of itself is enough for me, probably."

8

Reclaiming Democratic Literacy, Cautiously

In the field of education, a vast literature on democratic education exists that, like its authors, presents a wide spectrum of ideological beliefs and pedagogical practices. Some educators view democratic literacy as part and parcel of functional literacy. After all, becoming a "good" citizen can mean learning to obey rules made by those in positions of power, be they parents, teachers, government officials, or corporate CEOs. Indeed, a democratic education that starts and ends with developing "personally responsible citizens" (Westheimer and Kahne 2002), who are virtuous and law-abiding, generally perpetuates rather than destabilizes the status quo. This approach contrasts with a democratic education that promotes "enlightened political engagement" (Parker 2003).

The latter, which I endorse in the rest of this chapter, advances participation in the civic affairs of local, national, and global communities as well as critical assessments and collective transformation of unjust social, political, and economic structures (Westheimer and Kahne 2002). This approach also challenges thin constructions of U.S. citizenship that focus on voting, obtaining a Social Security number, and serving as compliant consumers and clients (Young 1990; Apple 2001; Hibbing and Theiss-Morse 2002). In short, democratic education for social justice promotes the development of knowledge, skills, and dispositions that enable students to become "active and powerful social agents" (Dance 2002, 69) who weigh in on local and more global forms of self-governance.

This ideal requires a thriving public square, where people can gather to discuss the issues affecting their collective well-being. Such a space—whether place-based or virtual—cannot exist without citizens who are able to listen and learn from others' perspectives, articulate their own, and make informed decisions about issues that impact the common good. That is, students need to develop democratic literacy. The first part of this chapter highlights Margaret and Paul's efforts to develop these capacities in their students. Unfortunately, the story does not end there.

The second part of the chapter examines a problematic discussion about illegal immigration that erupted in Julia's classroom. This event reveals that classroom discussions can and do reinforce relations of domination in a historically racist, classist, sexist, and heterosexist society (Boler 2004). Moreover, it shows how speakers trying to dialogue across social positions in a hierarchically ordered society (Wynter 2006) risk perpetuating institutionalized oppression. In part, this danger prevails because individuals from dominant groups often have "no ears to hear" (Jones, in Parker 2006, 15) speakers from marginalized groups. The discussion about illegal immigration epitomizes the need for educational programs that actively address this problem and strive for a more robust version of democratic literacy. I end the chapter with some suggestions for how schools, individual teachers, and the larger community can promote meaningful classroom discussions about controversial social issues that also preserve the personal safety and dignity of students from historically disadvantaged groups.

Before turning to the teachers' classrooms, I present another compiled dialogue from our monthly study group meetings. This dialogue both provides the teachers' rationales for using particular democratic educational strategies and exposes how differences in their educational settings both impede and support the development of democratic literacy.

The Role of Discussion in a Democratic Classroom

PAUL: I think that teaching discussion skills is just as much a part of the curriculum as the content we teach. Because grades are not important at Lakeside, we can be really responsive to social issues. A well-established part of our classroom is talking about difficult issues, and we teach skills about how to conduct discussions on them. For example, we work on saying what we know and don't know about a particular issue and where we got our information.

MARGARET: I did my Socratic Circles project precisely because my students did not know the rules for engaging with other citizens in formal public discussion, and the Socratic Circles model had very clear parameters. Students need to be taught skills about what is and is not okay to say in a classroom environment.

PAUL: To me, a crucial part of democracy is taking on different issues through discussion before doing informed decision making based on our sharing and negotiation. I stay at Lakeside because I can work with the students to create a democratic classroom there. Student-facilitated discussions, like the videotaped one that you all watched about the quality of life at Lakeside, is a regular part of our schedule. We have a sheet of paper on which any member of the classroom, including teachers, can suggest a particular discussion topic. We also assign a facilitator for each discussion, and the students know that as the facilitator they are not supposed to dominate the conversation but, instead, keep it going and maybe make summarizing statements about it.

MARGARET: Was the behavior we watched in that morning meeting pretty typical, Paul? I'm not talking about content, but just your students' social behavior—the way they sat and their level of engagement. Was that a particularly good meeting? Because I was impressed by the way your kids were acting. I mean camera on them or not, I would die a happy woman if most of my classes looked like that, even seventy percent of the time.

PAUL: The kids will usually sit more quietly for me than for my co-teacher when I start the morning meeting, and I think the videotaping was a moral regulator for some of the kids. But it's not unusual for a serious subject like that to be not quite as lively. For some topics, there are more interruptions, and the student facilitator will get frustrated and say, "Shut up!" quite a bit.

JULIA: They were certainly very courteous in the video clip.

PAUL: They were, but there is quite a range. Still, my students do have the opportunity to practice this discourse style for years.

JULIA: That videotaped conversation ended with no resolution in sight, but nobody's voice was even raised. So many of my students have no threshold for frustration. They just flip into this angry, confrontational mode because that's the only way they know how to resolve things. They yell about it, scream about it, and maybe physically work it out. Many of my students just don't have the skills to really talk through something.

MARGARET: I know. Nobody threatened anybody in Paul's room. I loved that. Do you think that the regular forum of your morning meeting helps to build a strong community, Paul? That it enables your students to work through inevitable social struggles that will continue into adulthood?

PAUL: I think so. The social discourse that takes place not only during the meeting but also in the informal interactions and problem solving throughout the day is the substance of life in a lot of ways. For me, this education is messier but that is what democracy is, too. It takes time and is complicated and confusing at times. Why shouldn't kids start learning those skills, practicing them, and dealing with social issues at a young age?

Some people, however, have a sort of tough love, authoritarian viewpoint. I've mentioned before that there's a huge debate about whether Lakeside's version of democratic education is appropriate for all kids. I don't have enough experience with your kids, Margaret, to know if these folks are right, but I was in a middle school in Boston years ago that had an open classroom like mine. The teacher took all of the really tough kids, and the open classroom seemed to be working for them. Most of the other teachers, however, felt that the school needed to be essentially like a military academy.

JOE: Some kids need that.

MARGARET: Yeah, I've seen a lot of kids do well in a structured environment and then fall apart in my classroom. One of the teachers in my building runs a class where the fences, the boundaries, are set in cement with twenty-foot-deep posts. For kids whose lives are in a constant state of chaos, his classroom is the one place every day where they feel safe. As much as that grates against kids who need more freedom, a lot of kids don't need any more turmoil in their lives. I've come to appreciate that this teacher is good at creating a very safe intellectual and emotional environment.

Even so, knowing your job as a teacher at my school usually translates into exerting enough control to make all of the students' peripheral behavior, or as much of it as possible, disappear. We're supposed to be spending our time talking about *Oedipus Rex*, and that's it. There's the expectation from a lot of quarters in my building that dealing with the social stuff is a waste of time. But I don't see that as a waste of time. Problem solving is messy and difficult, and problems are sometimes not resolved, but I saw Paul's kids doing what I have tried very hard to teach my kids how to do this year. That morning meeting was impressive and is what I think people ought to be doing with middle school kids.

The reason I did Socratic Circles was because my kids were not talking to each other, and I found that after doing them, my classes were a lot more interactive. But I had to do a lot of training to get them to that point. When I watched the video of me teaching at the beginning of this school year, I saw that the class was ninety-five percent about me—I was the star of my own show. That video reminded me how hard I have to work to get my kids to a spot where they are able to take ownership of and leadership in the classroom.

JULIA: I think it's interesting that focusing on the quality of social interactions is part of the agenda—part of the philosophy—at Paul's school, whereas at Margaret's and my schools, if you choose to address students' behavior, you are supposedly taking time away from the curriculum that you should be teaching.

MARGARET: Right. The kids you are talking about, Julia, who are so angry and aggressive. How different would their lives be now if when they were eleven and twelve years old, somebody spent all those hours teaching them the language and the skills that they needed to do something besides punch somebody in the face? Just the way your room is laid out, Paul, demonstrates how important democratic social interactions are. With Socratic Circles, I did a little run into your world, but it was an event, whereas it's a way of life in your classroom.

PAUL: Well, you have asked before, Margaret, if you could do with your kids what I do in my classroom. No, you could not. Most of my kids already have a lot of negotiation skills and knowledge that will help them in the dominant culture. But, with the Socratic Circles, you are teaching your kids to participate positively in a form of democracy that we want. I think you are being incredibly courageous to try to get this kind of stuff happening where you are.

MARGARET: Well, it doesn't always work. I've had to move one of my classes back into rows. I can't seem to get that group of kids to self-regulate in more socially appropriate ways because they see my lack of willingness to assert power as a sign of weakness. I have to constantly remind them that, in fact, I do have power, know how to use it, and will.

Interestingly enough, I am more naturally inclined toward your style of teaching, Paul—of not being a disciplinarian. But that does not fly with a lot of my kids or their parents. When I first started teaching at Johnson, some parents downright accused me of being weak. If I could not show these kids who was boss, what the hell did I expect? I need to be really clear about expectations and boundaries with my students in a way that would not be tolerated at Lakeside. It was a brutal wake-up call to find myself as a middle-class white lady in a roomful of children whom I knew nothing about, who quite clearly did not like me, and who had parents who would just as soon I drop dead as teach their children.

So maybe the problem is me. I don't know where the acceptable line of authority is with some kids, so I'm constantly making mistakes when I'm telling them what they can do. Maybe I'm not explaining clearly to them where those lines are because I don't understand the students and their out-of-school culture well enough. I understand it superficially, as an observer, but that is not the same thing as living in it and really knowing its rules.

PAUL: Do the students know in advance that you're planning to run the class differently? Because if they can think in advance on it, maybe when they walk in they will be prepared for what's going to happen in terms of the classroom's format.

MARGARET: Yeah, they know that, and the Socratic Circles worked fine with that particular group. Where I got into trouble was trying to incorporate democratic procedures into the daily business of class. I could not drag the authority line back and give those students more power, and I have not ever been able to figure out what it is that I did wrong.

JOE: My sense is that with certain students, it isn't enough to say, "Okay, we're going to be conducting Socratic Circles next Tuesday." I could have said it in Chinese, and it would have gone just as deep because they are only responding to stimuli occurring at this moment. In some contexts, there's no better way to operate. But in a classroom context, it's problematic.

MARGARET: So what do you do? How do you help them make that shift so they can negotiate a social situation that isn't the street?

JOE: What it requires, in my opinion, is incredibly small groups and an awful lot of attention.

MARGARET: Like Paul's school, where there's an intense community for a long period of time?

JOE: Half that population though. The numbers have to be that small.

JULIA: I think it's interesting, Margaret, that you feel like an outside observer of your students' community who does not understand what you need to be doing differently. Your students are in the exact same situation. They are thrown into this classroom environment, but doing school is not instinctual to them. How can we make school theirs enough that they take responsibility for it and their behavior?

PAUL: Even with the kids in my school, I'm constantly having to measure what structure kids need, and it's different for each kid, depending on who they are and where they are on any given day. It's constant observing, adapting, stepping in during certain situations, and still trying to be consistent and fair with all of them. Running a democratic classroom is hard work, even when it is the regular mode of operation.

MARGARET: That is definitely not the operating mode for my kids. I have had near riots in my room because they can't handle the freedom of the expanded space or renegotiate their positions. One of my constant concerns is not jeopardizing my children's physical safety.

PAUL: I've found that you have to work to get to that point where you are running an effective open classroom that offers a safe learning environment. If it's too loose, and the kids are confused, forget it. Then you're doing harm. Plus, our small group of students is together all the time in my school setting. And I should say that there are kids who fail in my classroom environment. We try to be honest that our open classroom is not for everybody and add structure for kids who need more of it. A couple of kids are going to public middle school next year, largely with our blessing, because Lakeside is not working for them. Still, I think we too often do not respect childhood as a time for all kinds of rich adventures and forms of existence that exceed sitting in a desk and taking a test.

Developing Democratic Literacy via Classroom Seminars and Deliberations

During study group discussions like the foregoing one, the teachers identified the following critical attributes of a democratically literate classroom: nurturance of the common good, nonviolent conflict resolution, and/but the recognition of conflict as essential to a robust democracy, wherein the sharing of diverse, seemingly incompatible views returns decisions that better serve everyone in the long run. Both the seventh-grade Socratic Circles described in Margaret's portrait and daily student deliberations in Paul's classroom fostered these qualities.

The Socratic Circles that Margaret so carefully set up enlarged student understanding of an academic text (the article on single-sex school debates) and each other (Parker 2006, 12). They also interrupted the entrenched linkage between doing school and obeying teacher orders by quietly completing individual seatwork (Tyack and Cuban 1995). During the Socratic seminars, students worked to "develop and clarify observations, meanings, and analyses" on an intellectual topic not in spite of but through their peer-to-peer interactions (Parker 2006, 13). As a consequence, many students took more active roles in facilitating subsequent classroom learning activities, and Margaret's role changed, becoming more facilitative and less directive. Paradoxically, however, this shift from authoritarian figure to "active co-learner and facilitator" (Antrop-González and De Jesús 2006, 423) required some directive, skills-based teaching.

As noted in chapter one, Margaret explicitly taught her students the social behaviors expected in formal, public discussions. Once the students understood the social significance of a more structured discussion and acquired the tools to carry one out, Socratic Circles provided them an avenue to practice public discussion skills and take responsibility for their own learning. Additionally, the discussion on a controversial public issue—whether or not our democracy should endorse single-sex schools—pushed students to reflect critically on biological and social claims about gender. Paying attention to their own beliefs and those of their peers helped students learn more about the topic and revise their own perspectives when they were based on faulty or groundless assumptions.

Although an effective discussion strategy, Socratic Circles do not foster the "action-in-the-world" (Parker 2006, 13) component of democratic literacy. In other words, text-based seminars like Socratic Circles illuminate an issue but do not demand that students make a decision about a shared problem. Accordingly, deliberations need to complement student-centered seminars in the quest for a robust democratic literacy (Parker 2006). By deliberation, I mean collectively "weighing alternative courses of action and trying to *decide* which policy would be best for all concerned" (Parker 2003, 80, my emphasis). Importantly, the decision-making aspect of deliberation links directly to social justice, as a democratic literacy aimed at challenging rather than sustaining the status quo must go beyond thinking about an issue if it is to effect change (Anyon 2005; Westheimer and Kahne 2002).

Like Margaret's Socratic seminars, high-quality deliberations do not occur fortuitously. They require the ongoing development of particular knowledge, skills, and dispositions. In the context of my study, such deliberations took place during the morning meetings in Paul and his co-teacher's classroom. Nearly every school day, students formed a circle and deliberated an issue of common concern. As Paul explained in the previous dialogue, classroom members selected the morning meeting topics, and students generally facilitated the deliberation.

In addition to deliberating an unsatisfactory classroom climate, the students addressed the mysterious disappearance of personal belongings, the exclusion of girls from recess football games, and uncertainty about hanging a "safe space" poster, designed to display the acceptance of and support for lesbian, gay, bisexual, transgendered, queer and/or questioning (LGBTQ) individuals, on the classroom wall. Regarding the latter example, the students decided that the room was not yet a safe space; the classroom community needed to do more work before it could hang the poster with integrity. Although the students did not always resolve issues during the morning meeting deliberations, through the process of "finding and weighing alternatives and deciding among them" (Parker 2006, 12), they considered what policies and practices best served their learning community—not just themselves—and successfully worked through conflict via talk. Additionally, as Paul emphasized in the foregoing dialogue, they grew accustomed to the complexities and controversies that attend "the actual political community we inhabit" (Hess and Stoddard 2007, 236). By regularly participating in deliberations, Paul's students also acquired valuable negotiation skills that will benefit them in the institutional spaces of the "culture of power" (Delpit 1995), such as workplaces, city halls, and courtrooms. More specifically, they practiced identifying and naming a problem publicly and learned how to use reasoned arguments and persuasive evidence when discussing resolutions to that problem.

Importantly, however, Lakeside's private status shielded students from contemporary accountability measures, like *No Child Left Behind,* that do more to promote "market competition, privatization ... and punitive measures" than democracy and social justice (Michelli and Keiser 2005, xvix). In their small school, Paul and his co-teacher had access to ample resources and time, both of which they used to create engaging, interdisciplinary curricula. Unlike Margaret, who taught fifty-minute classes each day over a nine-month period, Paul and his co-teacher spent almost the entire day with the same group of students for three consecutive years. Lakeside's structuring of informal and formal interactions among students and teachers over this extended period of time enhanced "students' active engagement" and "a sense of community among students" (Antrop-González and De Jesús 2006, 419). Moreover, the majority of students came from middle- to upper-middle-class homes, with parents who held advanced degrees. As Paul noted in the previous dialogue, his kids already possessed the knowledge and skills that dominant institutions expect and reward. Indeed, his students, unlike Margaret's, had practiced deliberations and other "legitimate" forms of discussion at home and at school since they were young children.

The stark differences between Margaret's and Paul's classrooms reveal the limits of achieving social justice through school-based democratic literacy in today's world. Unfortunately, "[p]ublic goods [including schooling] are no longer broadly and equitably available, but instead constituents must be well-informed, industrious, and 'entrepreneurial' enough to demand and search out the best public services" (Pattillo 2007, 179). With enough money, these savvy adult constituents can send their children to a private school like Paul's, where democratic practices are the norm rather than the exception. Importantly, learning to facilitate and participate in meaningful public discussions on controversial issues requires diligence, practice, and, thus, ample opportunities for discussion (Hess 2004). Teachers and students in school settings with rigidly narrow curricula, little time and money, and/or restricted access to linguistic and social codes of power (Delpit 1995) rarely have such opportunities. As Margaret stated starkly during our tenth study group meeting,

> If I felt I wasn't a good teacher ... I think I would take heart from that because I would feel that I could get better. But I can never be good enough to give most of my students what they need because I've got an intractable system that's working against me ... I've thought a lot about ... what we ask kids to do to be successful in the educational system. But I don't know that I can ask kids to try to change this system because I don't feel like I can do it. I'm a grown-up woman with some resources—I've got a lot of capital, social and financial—but I feel like I can't do anything except get out and run away.

Nevertheless, we as educators can focus our energies on interrupting the pathways by which macro-level structural inequalities in U.S. society seep into our psyches and classrooms. Even in Paul's educational setting, a model for developing students' competent "participation in a self-determining political community" (Parker 2006, 11), traces of deep-seated prejudices and power inequities, learned from other institutions like the family and media, regularly interfered with his quest for social justice. We as educators, then, have ample work to do on our local learning communities and ourselves if we are to identify, confront, and transform social injustices occurring in our own backyard.

Because educators are themselves curricula in that "who [we are] plays a significant role in what [we teach] which plays a significant role in what the students learn as part of the curriculum" (Finnessy 2007, 6), we can decide to confront or ignore "historically and socially determined inequities" (Boler 2004, 11) in our classrooms. In the remaining pages, I use a teachable moment from Julia's classroom to argue that the ever-present danger of conducting classroom discussions "in which entrenched inequalities proceed as usual" (Parker 2006, 15) should not stop us from trying to challenge those selfsame entrenched inequalities in K–12 educational contexts.

Running Toward Troubling Teachable Moments

On a late spring morning, while I was filming Julia's freshman study skills class, an informal conversation about illegal immigration erupted. That day, the normally small study skills class was even tinier. Only three students, Julia, and I were present. The discussion began when Brittany, a multiracial female student, asked Julia if she thought the nearly all-white Hancock School District was diverse. Julia responded that the Latino population had grown significantly since she began working in Hancock. Brittany then whispered loudly, "That's because half of them aren't supposed to be here," prompting Scott, a white male student, to announce, "I think we should shoot all the illegals."

Julia asked Brittany and Scott to support these and additional assertions ("*We* give *them* our taxes"; "*They* stab people"; "*They* sell illegal drugs") with sound reasons and evidence. I burst in to emphasize that many undocumented workers also pay taxes, without reaping the rewards, and frequently do the nonunionized, low-wage labor that most U.S. citizens seek to avoid. After Brian, the other white male student in the classroom, highlighted that white people took the land from indigenous peoples, Julia emphasized that everybody in the room had migrated to the United States at some point and that *white person* and *U.S. citizen* were not synonymous, as Scott had suggested. Knowing that the students were studying imperialism in their U.S. history class, I also asked if *we* were implicated in other countries' poverty. Brittany replied by attributing the U.S. problems to George W. Bush. When the bell rang moments later, the conversation ended and was not revisited before the school year ended.

During the study group meeting when we watched a videotaped version of this discussion, Julia asked:

> Where do you fit in these big things when they come up? Do we just stop everything? Where does our commitment lie? If you do take an issue and run with it, what is the goal? Do you want to have an educated conversation, because in [the immigration] discussion I felt like the students' parents were standing behind them, and they were just mirroring and echoing opinions they have heard elsewhere. They are not speaking from a place of having studied or thought deeply about immigration. Where do you go with that?

The rest of this chapter tackles her questions.

A Rationale for Interrupting and Working Through Hateful Speech

Although the immigrant discussion took place in one classroom and, thus, cannot be extrapolated to the larger world of K–12 education, it reaffirms a nationwide fear of the "illegal alien." The mayor and city council's September 2006 passage of the "Illegal Immigration Relief Act" in Hazleton, Pennsylvania, poignantly captures such fear. This ordinance, designed to punish local residents who hire or shelter illegal immigrants, emerged after undocumented workers perpetrated two violent crimes. According to Hazleton's mayor Louis J. Barletta, "When you start seeing … very violent crimes being committed and time and time again those involved are illegal aliens, it doesn't take a brain surgeon to figure out that you're experiencing a problem here that you've never had before" (Kroft 2006).

Scott's claim that "[illegal immigrants] stab people" echoes Barletta's inflammatory statement. Indeed, both support long-standing nativist discourses—a "defensive nationalism" (Cornbleth and Waugh 1995, 6)—about who is and is not a true (white) "American" citizen. The immigrant discussion thus signals a terrified response to the largest influx of immigrant students, many of whom are not white, Christian, and/or native English speakers, into U.S. urban *and* suburban classrooms since the beginning of the twentieth century (Banks 2006, ix). This reaction is unsurprising in the U.S. context, where we consciously and unconsciously strive to keep our deep-seated history of white supremacy a "cultural secret" (Berlak 2004) and obscure entrenched inequalities by teaching only "official knowledge" (Apple 2000) in many public schools.

Returning to the specificities of the immigration discussion, although Julia asked Scott to justify his violent statements with evidence, I found myself wanting to silence him, or, more accurately, to take away his discursive weapons and try to persuade him of the decidedly real harm that language can do. These divergent responses—allowing versus prohibiting hateful speech in the classroom—strike at the heart of democratic literacy, as they expose seemingly incompatible positions on the teacher's role in regulating words and actions.

In our monthly study group discussions, Margaret and Julia expressed legitimate fears about indoctrinating or silencing young students if they shared their own political views during classroom discussions of controversial issues. However, attempting to remain neutral in the face of comments like Scott's sends the message that both his speech and existing inequities involving undocumented workers are acceptable. Accordingly, such an approach does not advance social justice (Bender-Slack and Raupach 2006). As James Garrison argues, "There are no neutral matrices allowing us to escape our cultural inheritance, although the dominant discourse of modern liberalism assumes there are" (2004, 91). In other words, the refusal to acknowledge openly historically formed, systemic inequities impedes efforts to challenge them (Boler 2004; Delpit 1995). Sound reasons thus exist for ensuring substantial protections for all students through the disruption of not only discriminatory speech but also "official silence" about enduring institutionalized discrimination against particular social groups (Mayo 2004).

More specifically, Scott's violent statement merits interruption and critical analysis in the classroom so as to protect the personal safety and dignity of students from minority culture groups, particularly because most of those students are compelled by U.S. law to attend school. If we situate Scott's violent speech within a history wherein all voices have not been recognized equally and, more directly, his white male voice has "been permitted dominant status for the past centuries," we have legitimate reason to suppress his speech (Boler 2004, 13). However, halting his hostile claims is only the beginning of the story. To prevent Scott from becoming a "tourist of inequality" (Mayo 2004) and to resist reducing him to one more toxic label (Ayers 2006), the dialogue across differences must continue (Parker 2006). In short, affirmative educational processes that ask Scott to take responsibility for his ignorance more effectively encourage learning and community than the policing of his words (Mayo 2004). If we need "Band-Aids and stitches" to heal injustices, as I heard a colleague recently say, these processes ought to include immediate individual responses as well as long-term institutional ones.

Useful Band-Aids

How might an educator effectively respond to Scott's hateful commentary in that teachable moment? Because growth, change, and the creation of safe educational communities involve facing our vulnerabilities and the less satisfactory elements of our narratives (Bloom 1996; Garrison 2004), I begin this examination of in-the-moment responses to injurious speech by confronting the embarrassment and shame I experienced upon reliving and writing about the videotaped illegal immigrant conversation.

Walter Parker (2006) wisely recommends three strategies for "listening across difference" that link directly to my participation in the immigration discussion: humility, caution, and reciprocity. Briefly, humility involves recognizing our own views as incomplete, caution consists of moving slowly so as not to inadvertently offend or dismiss the validity of the speaker's perspective when speaking, and reciprocity centers on attempting to take the perspective of the other while recognizing that the speaker understands better than I "his or her social position, emotions, beliefs, and interpretations" (16).

In hindsight, I handled the pedagogical opportunity presented by the immigration discussion without adequate attention to these listening strategies; I particularly lacked caution. Scott's violent statements sparked a reactionary response from me—"They also clean toilets!"—a statement that ultimately reinforced harmful racial stereotypes and fostered an "us/them" mentality. Despite my intention to make Scott and Brittany think more deeply about the significant contribution that undocumented workers make to the U.S. economy, I opened the door to Scott not only laughing at my comment but also strengthening the overgeneralization by saying, "And [they] mow lawns." I thus fortified the notion that many undocumented workers are in low-paying, unprotected jobs not because of global economic conditions or punitive U.S. immigration laws but because they are incapable of being something more than "low-skilled, compliant, docile, pleasant, obedient service sector workers" (Gutstein 2006, 10).

Moreover, my sarcastic questions about the U.S. innocence in relation to the economic instability experienced by billions of people (Fraser 1997)—"Do you think we have anything to do with the poverty in other countries? Are we totally innocent?"—served mostly to silence the students. My arrogance and inability to understand the base of knowledge on which their statements were made did not shift the discussion from scapegoating undocumented workers to examining critically the U.S. and Europe's long-standing role in the colonization, marginalization, and exploitation of people around the globe. My pedagogical regret, however, ends there. Regardless of his motivations, Scott did great violence to undocumented workers when he proposed their extermination, and he did so in a formal educational setting, not the street. My intervention was faulty, but challenging his speech was an ethical imperative (Ayers 2006).

What might a more effective, long-term working through of Scott's and Brittany's injurious words require?

Committing to Stitches and Tackling Broken Bones

To confront our ignorance about the workings of social inequality, we need not only to learn *about* the forces driving illegal immigration, from a distance, but also to examine the feelings that "illegal aliens" evoke within us (Britzman 1998). As Margaret said after watching the videotaped footage of the immigration discussion, "There was a lot of fear in that room about all kinds of stuff. I kept wishing that was my class so I could ask the students what they are afraid of." To face, mourn, and transform our investments in institutionalized oppression, we all must find ways to identify and name the feelings of fear and/or shame underlying them (Berlak 2004).

Additionally, teaching approaches ought to address the intersecting nature and multiplicity of oppressions (Kumashiro 2008). Brittany's comments, in particular, raise the question: How should teachers respond when students from racial and/or other cultural minority groups also engage in oppressive and dominating speech? One possible response to Brittany's statements, which included, "Half of [them] use other people just so they can become a U.S. citizen," is to use a problem-posing pedagogy (Freire 1970/1994). Asking Brittany to answer some variation of the question, "What social institutions and values contribute to this being our learned response?" (Boler 2004, 12) would be a good way to make her think more deeply about the issue of illegal immigration.

As I emphasized in chapter four, threading stitches ought to help students name and understand institutionalized injustices, and their unique histories, without creating a hierarchy of "isms." According to Nicholas Burbules,

> A more multidimensional and relational view of difference ... would highlight the fact that dyadic dominant/marginalized, voiced/silenced, oppressor/oppressed relations are far too crude to capture the complex interdependencies of power operating in most classrooms, and would ask how all parties to an interaction of asymmetrical power contribute to that dynamic in various ways, and how they all need to reflect and change themselves if they are to challenge it. (2004, xxix)

As educators, then, we have a responsibility to help Brittany become accountable for her injurious ignorance, too.

As I also noted in chapter four, Joe's school, unlike Julia's and Margaret's, had an explicit code about student language. Indeed, his school replied with a resounding "No!" to the question: Should all speech be protected? More specifically, all students had to sign an antiharassment pledge. Joe's school sought to create a "space for students to develop their own voices" (Gutstein 2006, 32) that did not include verbal or physical harassment. However, this policy did not guarantee that speech offenders would take responsibility for their words or learn the historical precedents and institutional arrangements that made them possible (Mayo 2004). As Joe noted about the verbal antiharassment policy at his school, students sometimes used this policy to punish other students and teachers rather than to strengthen the school's learning community.

In many respects, Paul and Karen's classroom allowed for the most effective disruption and redressing of "the multiple workings of power" (Mayo 2004, 35). Yet, to reiterate a central claim in this book, their K–8 school's organization, particularly the long-term, intentionally structured informal and formal interactions among students and teachers, helped to create the kind of relationships that could withstand critical interrogations of the status quo. Thus central to a more robust democratic literacy are the conditions that allow schools as a whole—not just individual teachers, students, and administrators—to look long and hard at their school-wide policies and practices so that they can determine through a democratic process whether or not they are allowing institutionalized oppression to continue unabated, superficially limiting harmful individual speech and behavior, and/or substantively addressing the underlying reasons for both injurious speech and "official silence" (Mayo 2004, 34). In short, the cultivation of democratic literacy in the face of comments like, "I think we should shoot all the illegals," demands a considerable alteration of individual and collective practices, policies, and emotional investments.

Conclusion: Striving for Something Unachievable[1]

Despite having to work within repressive educational systems, teachers are not powerless (Gutstein 2006, 221), as Margaret's successful implementation of Socratic Circles in her classroom shows. Our troubled cultural heritage, however, means that teachers risk propagating social injustice if we refuse to acknowledge the conditions of alienation and domination that human-created hierarchies have engendered in the United States (Wynter 2006). To claim that we all come to the table as equals in the early twenty-first-century United States is to ignore our true inheritance (Boler 2004).

Moreover, being well meaning or even well reasoned is not the same as confronting one's own promotion of oppressions and doing the fundamental personal and institutional work required to heal the deep wounds they have forged and sedimented across centuries. In other words, using education to catalyze positive social transformation requires that all educational stakeholders relentlessly interrogate "accepted knowledges and approaches to them" (Scott 2005, 25). As Paul emphasized in the previous study group dialogue, teacher contributions to this work are messy and difficult. Important to sustaining beginning and veteran educators committed to social justice, then, is the recognition that anti-oppressive teaching involves unpredictability, partiality, and contradictions (Butin 2002; Kumashiro 2008).

Regardless of the unfinished nature of this work, those of us not being patrolled too closely by the "curriculum cops" (Kozol 2007) can employ teaching strategies that enable our students to speak and listen to one another and forge common ground. In addition to the seminars and deliberations mentioned in this chapter, resources abound for teachers who want to enact Structured Academic Controversies, town hall meetings, legislative hearings, fishbowls, and/or additional types of democratic forums in their classrooms (see, for example, Johnson and Johnson, 1995; http://www.crfc.org; http://www.choices.edu). Furthermore, educators can keep the democratic project moving in a positive direction by acquiring "broad social and disciplinary knowledge" and cultivating dispositions "to speak and open to one another" (Parker 2006, 16). Because the sources of this knowledge vary and are not agreed upon, deliberations about which of this knowledge to include in school curricula should include parents, community members, professional educators, and—I would add—students (Gutmann 1999). Accordingly, public contestation of undemocratic educational policymaking, including the textbook publishing machine and its general narrowing of what counts as "official knowledge," remains an important part of making these deliberations a reality (Apple 2000; Lipman 2004). Transforming dispositions, on the other hand, is work we can tackle both collectively and individually. After all, "[w]ar and peace start in the heart of individuals" (Chodron 2006, 16).

I therefore want to close this chapter by emphasizing the "relentless interrogations" that all of us—regardless of our social standing, prior knowledge, or institutional memberships—can commit to undertaking in the name of social justice. Summoning the courage to expose, question, and deconstruct our distortions of "Others" and our social reality is necessary for a more just construction of knowledge to take place (Finnessy 2007, 12). This uncomfortable labor holds the promise of moving us closer to "a society of citizens who admit that they are needy and vulnerable, and who discard the grandiose demands for omnipotence and completeness that have been at the heart of so much human misery, both public and private" (Nussbaum 2004, 17).

The ability to imagine a more inhabitable world for all of us fosters this rebuilding of hearts, minds, and institutions. I thus turn to visionary literacy in the final chapters.

PART V

VISIONARY LITERACY

9

Do Maggots Have Protein?

A Call for Visionary Literacy[1]

The Bravest—grope a little—
And sometimes hit a Tree
Directly in the Forehead
But as they learn to see—

Either the Darkness alters
Or something in the sight
Adjusts itself to Midnight—
And Life steps almost straight.
—*Emily Dickinson, "419"*

This chapter is a call for the courage and ability to visualize a different reality. Because a vision looks to the future, rather than the past or present, it necessarily involves groping and, thus, a willingness to face danger and uncertainty. Possibility is always accompanied by danger (Gutstein 2006), but we can choose to welcome this truth. After all, "Shadows make the light show" (Lamott 2005, 162). Or, to use a more apt metaphor for this chapter, maggots have protein.

Some may think that the ability to imagine a better story does not qualify as a literacy, particularly those heavily invested in protecting the "templates and schemata" (Greene 1995, 52) of our current social order, but I am arguing just that. In fact, I am claiming that visionary literacy involves three processes: developing a story for our personal lives and the world that we can not only tolerate but also desire; doing our best to realize that story through concrete, human, and, therefore, imperfect actions; and preparing for—even embracing—the maggots in life, as they are an inevitable part of this world and prevent us from forgetting that we need to keep pressing on. In short, cultivating a vision for social justice is not for the weak of heart.

Joe's storytelling during a class that I filmed brought both the metaphor of maggots and the concept of visionary literacy to life. I thus present excerpts of the study group discussion that centered on Joe's teaching and the teachers' approaches to helping their students conceive of an improved society and world. I then explore the connection between visionary literacy and social justice, using examples from the teachers' classrooms to strengthen my claims.

Maintaining Hope in a Difficult Time: Questing for the Fresh Peach

JOE: In my *The Impossible Will Take a Little While* class, we just read a Sherman Alexie essay called "Do Not Go Gentle" about the despair that he and his wife felt as they sat in a hospital waiting for their prematurely born child to die.[2] On his way home to take a shower one day, he decides to go into what he thinks is a toy store to buy something for his child. But when he walks in, he realizes it's an adult toy store. He doesn't want to seem like a prude, so he browses around and comes across a giant, black fifteen-inch rubber dildo called "Chocolate Thunder." He is so struck by the name that he buys it, runs to the hospital, and waves it over the child like a magic wand.

PAUL: Was he hallucinating?

JOE: No, he was just in such a state of despair that he needed something to lift him up. And everyone, all the other parents in the hospital, were laughing and grabbing the dildo and doing the same thing. But his child ends up pulling through, and his wife, to this day, swears that the child lived because of the energy that her husband brought into the hospital with that dildo. It's a great essay, and there are a lot of messages like that in the book. I bring up this story because I have this group of African-American kids who are really having a hard time engaging in the class. I'm fighting with them every minute and was really hoping this essay, because it is so funny, would strike a chord with them.

PAUL: I think bringing something into the lesson that is so disruptive to their logic that it stuns them can be useful. I am a bit of a Dadaist, but that kind of stuff helps so long as it is not too unsettling for them.[3]

Performance art that is odd or amusing enough can do that. Actually, the local group Diversity Stage is a good example. A group of high school students come into schools and observe kids, from kindergarten through middle school, and then write scripts about the conflicts they see, particularly those related to inclusion/exclusion issues. Something happens to these high school students as they undertake this project that is pertinent to dealing with social justice issues. Through this process of sharing their identities, feelings, and fears, these groups build an incredibly strong bond. Arts and theater have that power to some extent, and I think the kids who have done Diversity Stage will have big eyes, ears, and hearts around social justice issues wherever they go, for the rest of their lives.

JOE: Yeah, something heals or clicks for those students.

PAUL: I keep thinking about the personal story about peaches that we watched you tell your students, Joe, and its relationship to perseverance in the face of overwhelming adversity. Your students were totally captured by your quest for the perfect peach on a Southwestern reservation. Then to end the story with biting into a peach full of maggots...

JOE: The gross ending makes it fun and was too good to leave out. I have a reputation at school for telling stories.

PAUL: Storytelling builds a connection between you and the students. These little stories make up our lives. It is important for them to hear stories about us.

CONNIE: That reminds me of our discussion about what people think is appropriate curricular material. Would someone ask you, Joe, "What social studies or history content are they learning through your storytelling?" and not see the important engagement of and connection with your students that come out of it?

JOE: That particular story relates to a point in an Alice Walker essay that we were reading—that the existence of fresh peaches helps her get up in the morning.[4] So in that case, I would defend telling my story during class time.

PAUL: With any story, the students have to imagine where you were and think about spatial and human geography. There is a lot of social studies content in any storytelling. I do worry, though, about paralyzing kids with a lot of grim news. Kids need to understand what holds back social justice, but when you made that statement, on the video, about the cops always being right, I wondered if it contributed more to the kids' cynicism than to their sense of hope.

JULIA: Yeah, I don't know what your overall philosophy and goals for the class are, Joe, but in terms of students understanding how the bigger political picture affects their own personal lives and circumstances, are they able to get to a place where they can conceive of a future that is exciting or rewarding when they look at the world around them? I always thought about this question with my high school students, as many did not see a brighter future as a possibility.

JOE: Our school is definitely left of center in its tendency, which means we are very critical of the current social order, but I think there is a little more room for hope after the 2006 elections. Several kids also find things with which to become involved to feed them. I was really impressed by some kids who, on their own, went to New Orleans to help out after Hurricane Katrina during the winter break and again during the summer.

CONNIE: One thing I really appreciated in your classes, Joe, was that you presented illustrations of collective resistance—like showing that DVD of the Seattle protests against the World Trade Organization—that go beyond the exceptional American individual. In thinking about the development of hope rather than cynicism, I also saw the students become very engaged in your drumming class, in part because they were able to create something. This creative act seemed to inspire hope.

JOE: A lot of art classes allow students to distance themselves from the hard stuff. They can be creative instead of just reflecting on the world, which can be a very depressing place.

PAUL: That links back to the peach image. It's hard to resolve that a peach has this ineffable, wonderful quality that keeps me here, but I also might bite into one and find maggots there.

JOE: Well, isn't that a reflection of reality that kids should have? There are no guarantees that we are even going to live until tomorrow. Our future has not happened yet, so it's important to be as mindful and focused as you can on being who you are right now.

PAUL: But isn't that what the kids in the class were saying they are doing—living for right now?

JOE: Yeah, they say they live for the moment, but I think that is something they heard Tupac say and do not really understand what it means.

JULIA: As you were telling your story about the peach, Joe, I wanted to know what your students' peach is. Outside of everything else going on in the world, the peach is this tactile thing that you can taste and that has all of these pleasurable associations. So I wanted to know what gives your students pure joy. Then, as you talked about having a mouthful of maggots, this idea of taking risks, putting yourself out there, and being aware that even that essential core of what's good in life may not be exactly what you think it is, was really powerful. So then I wanted to know how that metaphor of the maggot-filled peach fits into their lives. I was also thinking about us as teachers—how do we get through the day-to-day when sometimes our peach is full of maggots? I mean, I am on peaches today!

Visionary Literacy: A Discussion

Walker's (2004) fresh peach metaphor and Joe's discovery that this ostensibly faultless fruit sometimes holds maggots seamlessly introduce this discussion of visionary literacy. As noted in this chapter's introduction, the work of social change requires both courage and hope. How can we gather courage in a world full of despair, violence, and inequality if we do not believe in the beauty of a peach or some other metaphor that can "tolerate the potency of desire, the thrust of diverse energies, the vitality of play, and the intention to transform" (Greene 1995, 52)?

In the previous study group conversation, I mentioned the imaginative power and fending off of hopelessness that Joe's drumming class invoked. I also observed this power in Paul's classroom where the integrated curriculum allowed students to explore a theme, like health, wellness, and human sexuality, through the lenses of multiple subject areas, including art and music. These curricular forms, as well as the aforementioned Diversity Stage program, stand in direct contrast to the technical demands of high-stakes standardized test preparation that require little imagination (Michelli 2005, 7). I elaborate briefly on a particular art center in Paul's classroom as well as a metaphor that Margaret introduced to her students through the reading of *Touching Spirit Bear* (Mikaelsen 2001) to illustrate the development of visionary literacy and to call for a renewed commitment to the arts, broadly defined, in education.

As I noted in Paul's portrait, students in his and Karen's classroom combined various clay hues to match their skin tones during the unit on genetics and diversity. This activity forced students to rethink the simple labeling of "black," "white," or even something more literary, like "café au lait," because the students created a representation of their skin with their own hands. In effect, it was not an activity aimed at imposition and control but rather an opportunity for the students to think critically about their own skin and simultaneously be released from the reductionist labels associated with race and ethnicity in this country (Greene 1995). Moreover, the activity did not end with these individual clay creations. Paul and Karen also asked the students to name their skin color, thereby inviting them to "participate [further] in the construction of their identities" (Grumet 1993, 206).

After the students created and named their clay creations, Paul and Karen made a mosaic hand of all the students' skin colors, creating yet another image of the possible—of something different from the conventional and routine (Elias 1995, 86). This time, the students' multiple skin hues were interwoven into a single, beautiful, definitively human sculpture. These creative acts, alone and in combination, enabled a vision of a pluralist democracy that isolated words in a book or even images and sounds in an already-made movie or song would likely not have realized. Importantly, however, the art center was accompanied by scientific, social, historical, and linguistic views of diversity and genetics. The students thus had the opportunity to think critically, functionally, *and* creatively about the unit and, in turn, potentially "transform the world to a degree, not in spite of but on the basis of given conditions" (Greene 1995, 51).

Maxine Greene's statement also relates directly to Margaret's teaching of literature. I always looked forward to visiting Johnson Middle School on the days that Margaret read aloud *Touching Spirit Bear* (Mikaelsen 2001) to her students. Despite her membership in the "largely hierarchical, bureaucratic" institution of Johnson, with its "internal demands for self-perpetuation and equilibrium," Margaret still found ways "for openings to be explored and critical thinking to take place" (Greene 1995, 56). She would ask questions that pushed the students to examine what they thought and why. In relation to *Touching Spirit Bear,* specifically, she asked them how they resembled and differed from the story's main character, who was not a praiseworthy individual. Indeed, Margaret's teaching of literature, whether she was using a modern-day fictional novel or a Greek tragedy like *Antigone,* always involved activities that linked the textual narrative to the students' own experiences and, in turn, our common humanity. I was lucky enough to be in Margaret's room the day she and her students discussed a metaphor much like that of the maggoty peach.

Touching Spirit Bear includes a lesson for the main character and reader that involves a stick. The right end of the stick represents happiness, and the left end, anger. No matter how many times you break off either end of the stick, the lesson goes, anger *and* happiness remain. "Life is what you make of it," Margaret told her students when discussing this stick. "What you decide to focus on becomes reality. Be brave and trust me that you are smart enough to do things on your own." As Margaret continued talking about the metaphor of life as a stick with her students, one of them earnestly said, "But you look at things differently, Ms. Nowak; you look deeply. I am not stupid, but to me, a stick is a stick."

I try to carry Margaret's reply to this statement with me everywhere I go: "Therein, my dear, lies the process of education, of looking through the eyes of someone who is not you ... Being educated means seeing things in a way that you did not see them before."

Conclusion

If, like Elisabeth VanderWeil (2007), we conceive of teaching as a celebratory affair, with its attention to creating a learning environment wherein we graciously accept what each guest brings, elicit and share stories, "assist with laying aside any unneeded outer layers," let our guests know what will be expected of them in this space, and stimulate engagement by taking risks and asking hard, honest questions, we are on the right track toward developing dispositions for social justice in ourselves and our students. Such capacities enable us to imagine forms of education that can contain each of our multitudes. To close this book, I explore the study group members' own visions of a more just educational system as well as our collaboration's contribution to social justice.

10

Conclusion

The Art of Cultivating Hope

> The ideal is knowledge, enlightenment, and truth on the one hand, and
> on the other, human freedom, emancipation, liberation. That this core
> of humanism is unachievable in some ultimate or final form can be dis-
> couraging to those whose mood is heavy, but it can also set a standard
> within the existential boundaries of our lived lives and provide, then,
> both focus and energy for our efforts.
>
> —Bill Ayers, *"Trudge Toward Freedom"*

Given my investment in privileging the teachers' perspectives throughout
this book, I conclude with one more edited transcript of our study group
meetings. This dialogue communicates the ongoing need for educators'
individual and collective visions of a more just and equitable social order.
In Ayers's (2006) terms, our study group calls for standards that stimulate
rather than deflate efforts to educate for social justice.

Our dialogue also speaks to the challenges of sustaining hope in this
historical moment when:

- A burgeoning number of U.S. high school students, particularly in
  the nation's largest districts where the students are predominantly
  African-American and Latino, are not graduating in four years
  (Kozol 2005), thereby increasing their chances of dropping out and
  entering prison (Meiners 2007);

157

- The increase in mandated, high-stakes, standardized testing in the United States is producing larger student retention and drop-out rates (Nichols, Glass, and Berliner 2005) and threatening to reduce education to the technical transfer of basic literacy and numeracy skills, particularly among the most impoverished youth (McNeil 2000b), of which there were 12.9 million in 2005 (U.S. Census Bureau);
- Many U.S. districts are rapidly resegregating (Orfield, Frankenberg, and Lee 2002) and will likely continue to do so given the U.S. Supreme Court's recent decision to forbid voluntary desegregation plans (Lowe 2007);
- More than 3.5 million English language learner youth were enrolled in U.S. schools (Suarez-Orozco 2001) as the government wrangled over and ultimately killed the passage of immigration laws in 2007, including the Dream Act, which would have helped an estimated 1.1 million young people who entered the country illegally as children obtain U.S. citizenship (Naylor 2007);
- Two-thirds of teens in a recent large-scale study reported that "they have been verbally or physically harassed or assaulted during the past year because of their perceived or actual appearance, gender, sexual orientation, gender expression, race/ethnicity, disability or religion" (Harris Interactive and GLSEN 2005, 3);
- A rapid rise in homeschooling—an estimated 1.9 to 2.4 million students were homeschooled in the United States during the 2005–2006 school year (Ray 2005)—as well as its deregulation, is undermining public education's ability to "bring children into social and intellectual contact with other children of diverse backgrounds" (Reich 2002, 172).

These trends do not bode well for a society that has not adequately addressed the suffering of its own poor and oppressed peoples—as evinced painfully by both the shameful pre–Hurricane Katrina preparations and post-hurricane fallout in New Orleans—let alone "the effects of our imperialism on the poor and oppressed peoples around the world" (West 2004, 19). Nevertheless, the teachers in this study continued to teach their students that our current reality is not inevitable. I thus present their shared wisdom on maintaining hope for a better tomorrow. I then close the book by examining this study's contribution to education for social justice.

Doing Our Best Within Context

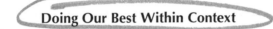

CONNIE: I remember a psychologist saying to me, "You social justice types try to take on the whole world, to your own detriment, because you wear yourselves down so much that you don't have any energy left to fight the world." I think it's a real balance to hang on to hope—to keep alive the idea of the peach without maggots—and maintain the will to continue facing the maggots, because there are a lot of them out there.

PAUL: Well, the nature of being a reflective teacher—knowing the condition of the world and that it needs to change—is that you never can do enough. I think it's very easy for conscientious, sensitive educators who are concerned about social justice issues to whip ourselves all the time. We can always say that we're failing because we kind of are. If you're going to be reflective about society, education, and what you do everyday, you sort of fail on a daily basis.

JULIA: I think it comes back to how we train our teachers. Some days, teaching sucks—you totally fail, or your coworkers undermine you. You may even have a whole semester where the dynamic in the classroom is terrible and you go home every day embarrassed and ashamed of yourself and your class. We set up so many teachers to fail because we do not structure in opportunities for us to talk about the huge issues that we deal with daily. Every once in a while, I would see glimmers of my high school students getting positive feedback and feeling really motivated. But I also saw other people pushing them back down. For so many of my students, their whole lives have been a training in resiliency. I guess the challenge is trying to refocus their *and* our energy so that school can serve as a place that generates positive experiences for the students and teachers.

JOE: I know that I've been feeling like I make very little difference. Part of me wishes the school day were longer or that I could open my home and be a foster parent for my whole school. We have such troubled kids, and I want so badly to be a catalyst in positively changing their lives. Still, talking about the concept of social justice through this group and the racial healing workshops I attend has gotten me beyond thinking about social justice and rather actively working to get inside the heads of my African-American students, which had not been happening much before. I am figuring out how to alter my teaching to meet their needs. It's an evolution.

PAUL: It's really important for teachers to have the time to sit together like this and just talk about daily life in the classroom. I get to do that often because I have a co-teacher with me almost all the time, and our school is small. Critiquing each other also becomes a natural part of our work because we're with each other so much. I'm in a really privileged situation, but even with all this support, I still want to talk about my work with teachers outside of my school. What we do is so complex that we need regular infusions of energy from others. I've gotten that from this group.

JULIA: On so many levels, I feel isolated at Hancock and one of the things that's been most valuable for me about this group is the opportunity it has afforded me to talk and think about how different each of our situations are—our students, schools, staff, and curricula—even within a ten-mile radius. In a way, this group has allowed me to step back and realize not only how different each classroom is, but also how different each teacher is. The idea has crystallized for me that what is "best practice" for one teacher may not fit for another, regardless of what the research says. Teaching is a process, and it's a really long process. I'm now somewhat comfortable saying it will take time for me to get to a place where I feel good about my teaching. I feel better knowing that you all have been teaching for a long time and are still struggling, changing, growing, and looking for more information. So I have a much better perspective on professional development—I see it as career growth rather than me being a failure if I do not make changes by tomorrow.

CONNIE: That actually reminds me of the feminist scholarship I have read. There is this common theme in that literature of striving for "good enough" practices rather than an unattainable ideal, which constantly leaves you feeling like a failure. What's hard about trying to develop a process-oriented approach in a world dominated by outcome-based models—like the state academic standards—is that if you say you are striving for "good enough" teaching, people see that as being complacent or not putting forth adequate effort. But I think we need to find ways to believe and say, "I'm trying my hardest, but I also have to be forgiving of myself so I can come back tomorrow and try again."

MARGARET: You know, I've been working with this boy Danny during the past year and a half, and he is one of those kids who just gets to me. I absolutely adore this child but see him come in and be so unhappy, demoralized, and overwhelmed by the stupid stuff that he has to learn. I recently looked at a history test that he has to take and was so disgusted that I almost burst into tears. It's a multiple-choice test about the difference between the Sugar Act and some other act. I don't know what the difference is and, quite frankly, I don't care. That test has seventy-five goddamned multiple-choice questions about bullshit, and somebody just got done telling me that my job is to help Danny pass it. When my teaching partner asked me to help her modify this test, I said I don't even want to talk about this test. So she sat down, all thirty years of her, and very sweetly said, "Margaret, let me explain something to you about this situation. I understand that there's an ideal world, but the reality of it is that we have to help these kids pass this test, and it's our job to do this." But I thought, no it isn't. If this is the reality of my life, then I'm getting out because this is not what I'm spending my life doing. I can't do this. I won't. I feel like Danny knows I'm a good teacher and that I have things to teach him about the Boston Tea Party, rebellion, what independence means, and fighting back. But my students are stuck in this system that cares whether they know the difference between the Stamp Act, the Sugar Act, and some weird thing called the Intolerable Act.

JULIA: But these kids will never leave the system. I don't mean to shove you farther down your hole, Margaret, but we are also stuck in this system. Whether it's the administration, the bureaucracy, or the fact that school funding mostly comes from local communities so the wealthy schools get all the money, when you think about the work you do with your students, you are one person whom they get to see every day who isn't so inculcated into this system that she can't even acknowledge it. You're someone who is frustrated by the system but who also loves your students for who they are, what they have, and what they bring to the classroom. How often do they see that during the day? You can't leave public education. I mean, you can leave if you need to leave, but I also think you need to recognize that you might be their little ray of sunshine in the middle of this hellhole. This group has provided an opportunity to recognize that we're stuck in this bigger machine over which we have very little control. When you actually step back, look at it, and think about all the ways you can't change it, you can get so depressed and stuck. But here are other voices of people who care, and, I don't know, it's inspirational. It keeps me going.

MARGARET: I always prided myself on understanding how the system works, accepting that certain things are the way they are, and moving on. Maybe this group put a chink in the belief that being mad at the system is like being mad that the sun comes up and then goes down every day. I'm not mad at some new weird thing that happened in my school; I'm mad at stuff that I've been dealing with for twenty years. But I've really confronted things recently that I spent a lot of time not paying any attention to because I was afraid that line of questioning would stop me dead in my tracks. Part of why I don't want to talk to my kids about social justice too much is because I don't want them to feel so overwhelmed by systemic problems that they become paralyzed.

PAUL: But the personal connections you are making, Margaret, are something to bring it all back to. What's most important ultimately is the quality of your interactions with the kids you see every day. A lot of us probably went into education because we wanted to make a difference in the world and so entered into this profession already socially aware. But maybe making the world a better place involves strengthening those daily connections that we have with each other and our students, connections that are honest, meaningful, kind, hopeful, and give meaning and value to living every day. The longer I live, the more I know that's the case. Our daily functioning has a lot to do with social justice. Do we live a good, healthy life and do the best we can? I'm deciding I don't like the phrase "good enough," because as a public statement, it does not send the right message to people outside the world of teaching.

JULIA: We could call it "doing your best within context." How about that?

Implications of This Study for Social Justice (Education)

Together students and teachers, researchers and subjects explore, inquire, investigate, search, ask questions, criticize, make connections, draw tentative conclusions, pose problems, act, seek the truth, name this and that phenomenon, circle back, plunge forward, reconsider, gather steam, pause, reflect, reimagine, wonder, build, assert themselves, listen carefully, and speak. It doesn't end.

—*Bill Ayers, "Trudge Toward Freedom"*

If nothing else, this book reveals the extent to which institutional context matters in the struggle for social justice. In many respects, comparing the education occurring in Paul's classroom to that in Margaret's is like comparing apples and oranges. Apart from the obvious similarities—both qualify as middle school education, are focused on teaching and learning, and involve white teachers—they share few characteristics. The physical layout of their classrooms, socioeconomic and cultural backgrounds of the students, school missions and histories, curricula, and teacher-student interactions differ dramatically. Accordingly, Paul's and Margaret's approaches to teaching for social justice, if they are to be effective with the specific groups of students they teach, must differ as well.

Although cultivating all the literacies presented in this book (functional, critical, relational, democratic, and visionary) is important for a robust form of socially just education, the current educational system's inequities mean some literacies are going to matter more than others in particular school settings. Given the increased options and rewards that accompany educational credentials in this society, for example,

Margaret should and does focus on developing her students' advanced functional literacy skills in a school marred by subpar standardized test scores. Additionally, considering the issues that many of Joe's students face, including drug addiction and run-ins with the criminal justice system, we should not underestimate the power of his caring. Indeed, his love for his students and deep understanding of their lives increases the likelihood that they will remain in high school and obtain the support they need to stay off the streets and out of prison.

I would commit a grave injustice, however, if I ended this book with an emphasis on contextual particularities. Paul's repeated claims that he could not teach his form of democratic education in Margaret's school and Margaret's growing frustration with teaching at Johnson are rooted in the realities of an unjust social order. Given the long, deep history of white supremacy, xenophobia, and exploitation of laborers in this country, and the more recent global, neoliberal mandates to privatize social services like education (Hursh 2006), it comes as no surprise that Margaret, whose students are largely of color and from low-income families, is at her wit's end. As Jean Anyon (2005) argues, the systemic problems of urban education require more than attention to pedagogy, curriculum, and assessment. Indeed, when employment opportunities do not exist, the wealthy do not have to contribute significantly to social safety nets, and laws do not protect against "the economic discrimination of people of color," poverty rates grow, and those in poverty must attend to survival more than the quality of their children's education (Anyon 2005, 61). The danger of empirical studies that focus on the particular is that they can ignore or, worse, deny the larger social and economic forces that threaten to run roughshod over all of us.

I thus appeal to Anyon's (2006) call for "concerted public protest and organization" (25) and William Tate's (2006) claim that "critical commentary" has a serious role to play in the marketplace of ideas (258). In isolation, we cannot effect the kind of large-scale social and economic transformations necessary to grow muscles and tendons on the abstract, fragile bones of "social justice" and "democracy." Our collective struggles, however, need to be varied and fought on multiple fronts. Although not a large-scale social movement, the grassroots study group described in this book created a safe space for five educators to comment critically on our own and each other's worldviews and teaching practices and, perhaps most importantly, be heard as "agents and experts on [our] own lives" (Ayers 2006, 85). The study group also helped to fill a gap in the teachers' professional lives, particularly for Margaret and Julia, both of whom felt isolated in their school settings. As Margaret said to the group during our last official meeting, "Seeing education through your eyes has been really helpful to me. It takes it out of my own head."

The fact that the teachers did not work together in the same building on a daily basis also contributed to their willingness to reveal the less savory aspects of their lives and work. Unfortunately, when schools have not established a strong professional learning community, intra-building study groups can lead to teachers questioning each other's credibility rather than collaborating to resolve issues in their classrooms, schools, and the field of education more generally (Grossman, Wineburg, and Woolworth 2000). In contrast, our cross-institutional teacher community sought to support and defend public schools and teachers on a local level (Michelli and Keiser 2005) and, more specifically, keep a talented teacher, Margaret, from ceding her position in the world of public education.

This research project was ultimately my pride and joy and, as such, was not *essentially* teacher driven. Nevertheless, I worked hard to set up an educational environment that was flexible enough to allow each group member to pursue her and his individual interests. Although not a substitute for meaningful professional development activities in the teachers' individual schools and districts, this structured but improvisational approach to teacher education stands in stark contrast to mandatory, standardized frameworks that tacitly or explicitly devalue teachers' abilities to identify and create meaningful learning opportunities (Darling-Hammond and McLaughlin 1995). Julia's articulate words, spoken during our copresentation about this study at a teacher education conference, capture the meaning of this group for her:

We were able to create a powerful sense of community among the five of us. There was a sense of trust and respect that allowed us to feel safe as we revealed ourselves through video footage of our teaching, to expose our failings along with our successes, and to sift through the difficult questions that have few satisfying or uplifting answers ... I remember eagerly anticipating our district-wide meeting of the teachers, administrators, and counselors who worked with students who were identified as "at-risk." I was hoping for a forum for interpreting ideas and philosophies, for resources to help strategize about research and pedagogy relative to the particular needs of our students. I don't miss that committee, which turned out to be not much more than breakfast and a building check-in of current programming. It has only been in the process of reflecting on this project that I connected this group with what I was looking for at those district meetings. It is a place to air my doubts and to question the ways that I impact my students; a place to discuss and explore the ideas that shape who I am in the classroom and how I interact with each of my students. It also sustains … my passion for teaching through a visceral understanding that [my classroom] is exactly where I can offer the most to my students.

More institutionalized, formal professional development programs as well as the development of evaluative tools for those programs (Grant and Agosto 2008) are necessary for the substantial realization of teacher education for democracy and social justice. Additionally, a year did not present sufficient time for the study group to pursue collaborative curricular projects or delve more fully into the intersection of various oppressions—namely, racism, sexism, heterosexism, and poverty. In concluding this book, however, I want to celebrate the doing of this small-scale, less than ideal study (Maguire 1993, 176). Group members are continuing to meet on a monthly basis and developing an issue-based, service-learning project with the teachers' students.

Additionally, although I did not measure the effects of the study group on the teachers' classroom practices, they claim that it has made a difference. As Paul said during our tenth meeting,

> I'm more vigilant about the teaching of social justice issues in my classroom these days. When we talk about dates in history, for example, I'm always looking for pieces that I can relate to fairness, equity, bigotry, or violence. Almost everything that happens has some sort of social justice issue embedded in it. Even the invention of the ballpoint pen involves a controversy about who invented the first one and how it was patented.
>
> Then there's this issue for me based on where I teach, which is that a lot of my students have cultural capital and most of their families are doing pretty well economically. I'm therefore trying to look at the way I teach about social justice issues and see if I am enabling students to use knowledge about oppression to their own advantage rather than take it permanently into their hearts.

I do not know where we are going as a group or as individual educators, but, against the entrenched dictates of this society, I continue to embrace this project, the teachers in it, and myself as "works-in-progress … both incomplete and provisional" (Ayers 2006, 85).

My research project aspired to be humanities-based with its underlying belief that "people, within genuine dialogue, change their own minds" (Barone 2006, 227). It also sought "to *artfully* coax [people] into collaborative interrogations of stale, tired, taken-for-granted facets of the educational scene" (Barone 2006, 227, emphasis in original) by presenting a narrative with complex characters rather than a depersonalized, decontextualized guidebook to education for social justice. The beauty and peril of a more arts-based approach to research is that its "refusal to reach toward indoctrination" means it relies on the viewer/reader to engage in dialogue about educational possibilities (Barone 2006, 227). My faith in our human ability to speak *and* listen, if we only try, requires that I relinquish this work to you, the reader, and invite your response.

"Finite to fail, but infinite to venture."

—*Emily Dickinson, "115"*

Appendix

Study Methodology

Educational research is frequently conducted in a manner that creates a rift between the teachers working directly with youth and the university scholars, administrators, policymakers, and curriculum designers who largely shape the K–12 educational agenda (Apple 2000; Zeichner and Noffke 2001; West 2004). This study therefore sought to create an opportunity for a university-based researcher and small group of teachers to dialogue across time about the substantive meanings, implications, and promise of education for social justice. I approached our five-person study group as a learning community in which "[t]eacher expertise and experience is at the core of the inquiry process," and "every group member is encouraged to participate in the discussion and subsequent actions on a continuous basis" (Tirrell-Corbin and Cooper 2008, 13). I also sought to address the genuine concern that researchers usually benefit far more than the study participants in collaborative educational research (Ladwig 1991) by compensating the teachers in ways that they identified as meaningful (such as with university credits).

Study Participant Recruitment and Data Collection

The study began with my recruitment of four K–12 educators from the same county who had varied life and teaching histories and taught different subject areas in their diverse school settings. With the exception of Margaret, in whose classroom I was tutoring when the study began, I found the following teachers by asking people I knew in the university, local schools, and surrounding community to identify teachers working for positive social change. I then contacted multiple teachers until I found four teachers willing to commit to a twelve-month, collaborative research process.

After conducting in-depth, ethnographic interviews (Fontana and Frey 2000) with each of the teachers at the beginning of 2006, I observed every classroom for two to three hours on a weekly basis and organized monthly, videotaped two-hour study group meetings during the rest of the year. Drawing on Francois Tochon's (1999) work on "video study groups," I thought that visual and verbal cues would be helpful when trying to analyze the way that we made sense of each other's philosophies and practices. The five of us cocreated the monthly meeting agendas, which included observing and analyzing each other's teaching via videotaped footage (see table A-1 for our study group calendar). As the study group facilitator, I strove to provide "structure, order and valuable research information" without controlling, directing, or dominating the group (Tirrell-Corbin and Cooper 2008, 13).

Unfortunately, I recruited and lost Lanae, an African-American community-based educator, three months into the yearlong study. Upon her request, I drew up an official contract for her participation in the study that included financial remuneration for her female student empowerment program. However, Lanae was understaffed and overworked, and my study was an obvious thing to cut from her overflowing plate. Moreover, my research design, with its emphasis on individual educators, was inappropriate in a community center context where youth and adults strove to sustain a coherent, horizontal team (Heath and McLaughlin 1993). Singling out Lanae during the recruitment process prevented me from gaining other staff members' trust. In other words, before I began collecting data, I did not devote enough time and energy to becoming more than an outsider—a white, university-based one at that. Lanae also did not identify with the other teachers in the study (although she never met them) because she perceived herself as a social worker before a teacher, and schools as sites of social control rather than liberation. Her departure underscored the difficulty of bridging the institutional divides between universities, schools, and community-based organizations.

Table A-1. Monthly Meeting Dates, Topics, and Locations

Meeting Number	Date	Meeting Agenda	Location
1	January 29, 2006	Introductions, setting group norms, exploring project goals and activities	Connie's house
2	March 5, 2006	Sharing life histories	Joe's house
3	April 2, 2006	Sharing individual perspectives on social justice and education for social justice	Paul's classroom
4	April 30, 2006	Discussion of Connie's essay on approaches to social justice education	Margaret's classroom
5	May 21, 2006	Screening Paul's teaching and follow-up discussion	Julia's classroom
6	August 1, 2006	Screening Julia's teaching and follow-up discussion	University room
7	September 17, 2006	Beginning of the year check-in and discussion of a collaborative curricular project	Joe's house
8	October 22, 2006	Screening Margaret's teaching and follow-up discussion	Paul's classroom
9	November 12, 2006	Screening Joe's teaching and follow-up discussion	Coffee shop
10	December 17, 2006	Reflecting on study group experience, discussing possible future collaboration	University room

Data Analysis and Writing Methods

To analyze the study's data, I transcribed the initial interviews and monthly meetings. The interview transcripts, along with my field notes and classroom documents from the weekly school visits, became the backbone of individual teacher portraits (Lightfoot 1983; Lawrence-Lightfoot and Davis 1997). The five-literacy model emerged from my "selective open coding" (Emerson, Fretz, and Shaw 1995, 155) of the study group meeting transcripts and analytic memos that I wrote immediately after each meeting. To organize the data, I coded the transcripts with NVivo, a qualitative data software. Although this computer-based tool helped me sort the data, I—not the software—created the codes, associated them with text excerpts, and interpreted the coded data that emerged. To write the final narrative, I returned to my field notes and classroom documents to find school-based evidence supporting the five-literacy model and revised my initial analyses in response to the teachers' feedback.

The writing of compelling stories required that I adhere to narrative truth rather than factual accuracy when setting up scenes and dialogues (Ellis 2004). In other words, although I constructed stories that correspond as closely as possible to actual experiences, I altered the verbatim speech of the group members or myself when it interfered with the usefulness of the story (Ellis 2004, 126). Nevertheless, I sought to guard the meaning of each speaker's words and asked each teacher to verify that I appropriately represented his or her ideas. When I misinterpreted their truths, I revised the story. As I crafted the group conversation excerpts, I also intentionally juxtaposed competing standpoints whenever possible. In other words, the group conversations did not necessarily take place in the order they appear. A comment made in meeting nine might thus appear next to a comment made in meeting one. I played with the chronological order of statements because the surfacing of tensions holds the promise of rupturing taken-for-granted assumptions about educational processes and, thus, creating openings for positive social transformation. By exposing contradictions, I aimed to spur movement. Additionally, I infused parts of my personal story into the text because "[i]ncluding the subjective and emotional reflections of the researcher" can, when done carefully, "add context and layers to the story being told about participants" (Ellis 2004, 62). I leave it to the reader to decide how convincing and evocative that story is.

These writing methods trouble easy or fixed readings of the research process and the group members' stories, including my own. Because "[i]n any narrative, an evaluation from the narrator's point of view is always present, whether or not it is openly stated" (Kendall and Murray 2005, 748), I wanted to make evident my authorial role and include the viewpoints of the teachers when they had an elaboration, critique, or addition to make to my writing. Using other qualitative researchers as guides (e.g., Hollingsworth 1994; Segall 2002), I therefore integrated the teachers' commentary into the book. Additionally, I asked the teachers to provide individual representations of how this study group influenced their ideas and practices. We presented these commentaries at educational conferences and compiled them into an article, which is currently under review by an academic journal. As noted in the introduction, I also used poetry when I deemed it more powerful than prose. Depicting transcribed conversations on the page as poetic stanzas can more effectively capture the everyday speech of the research participants during interviews, focus groups, or other dialogic processes (Kumashiro 1999, 2002). Poems also prevent the reader from forgetting that the author has manipulated and edited what ultimately lands on the page (Kumashiro 2002).

I attempted to reduce the alienation of teachers and readers who have not been socialized into academic Discourses (Gee 1996; Collins 2000) by writing in clear, conventional prose. Nonetheless, I am mixing teacher and academic Discourses because neither—alone or in combination—captures human experience in its entirety nor disrupts commonsense notions that promote the domination and suppression of particular people's "cultural protocols, values, and beliefs" (Smith 1999, 5). My goal of making clear *and* complex claims in the written social critique that I present translates into a both/and approach with regard to using traditional academic writing alongside more experimental forms (Leonardo 2004, 14; Kendall and Murray 2005).

I write with "a deepened, complex, thoroughly partial understanding of the topic," knowing "there is always more to know" and that this text is a process, not a definitive representation (Richardson 2000, 934, 936).

Notes

Note for the Introduction

1. All teacher, student, and location (i.e., school, university, and city) names are pseudonyms.

Notes for Chapter 1

1. See Delpit (1995).
2. See Palmer (1998).

Notes for Chapter 2

1. A novel by Ben Mikaelsen (2001), *Touching Spirit Bear,* involves a fifteen-year-old who savagely beats his classmate and, in lieu of going through the traditional criminal justice system, is given the opportunity to participate in restorative justice via Native American Circle Justice.

2. Dr. Ruby Payne (2001) was a secondary teacher, elementary principal, and central-office administrator who wrote *A Framework for Understanding Poverty.* As the CEO of aha! Process, a training and publishing company, she has led numerous workshops on how to teach low-income students effectively.

3. See Paulo Freire and Donaldo Macedo (1987).

Notes for Chapter 3

1. See Jensen (2004).
2. See Manes (1990).

3. See Nystrand (1997).
4. See Tye (2000).

Notes for Chapter 4

1. According to a prominent sociologist at the University of Rockland, African-Americans are imprisoned at least eight times as often as European Americans in the United States, and in Rockland, specifically, the state incarcerated 4 percent of the black population in 2001, meaning that an average African-American person was 11.6 times more likely than a white person to be incarcerated in the state. A 2001 report from a policy institute also showed Rockland's African-American students to have a 40 percent graduation rate, whereas the state had an overall graduation rate of 85 percent.

2. Joe was participating in a local racial healing group, facilitated by a world-famous African-American jazz musician, which met weekly over a two-month period. The group sought to develop a dialogue on racism centered on listening to each other and viewing racism as a disease that causes everyone to suffer. For more information on this approach, see Newkirk and Rutstein (2000).

3. See Loeb (2004).

4. See Gutstein (2006).

5. On October 2, 2006, thirty-two-year-old Charles Carl Roberts IV entered a one-room Amish schoolhouse in Paradise, Pennsylvania, shot and killed five girls execution-style, and bound and critically wounded six other girls before killing himself. The girls were six to thirteen years old, and Roberts allowed the fifteen boys in the classroom to leave (CNN 2006).

Notes for Chapter 5

1. See Myers (1999), Spiegelman (1986), and Ehrenreich (2001), respectively.

2. See Glodoski (1998).

3. Tye (2000): 87.

4. See Mun Wah (1994), California Newsreel (2003); and Obidah and Teel (2001), respectively.

5. See Kunjufu (2002).

Notes for Chapter 6

1. See Noddings (1984).
2. See West (1984).

Notes for Chapter 7

1. See Ashby and Ohrn (1995) and Myers (1991), respectively.
2. See Avi (1991).
3. See Paley (1992).
4. See Noddings (1984).
5. See Teaching Tolerance's website (http://www.tolerance.org), Boal (1979), and Rennie Harris's website (http://www.rhpm.org), respectively.

Note for Chapter 8

1. This heading comes from Nussbaum (2004, 17).

Notes for Chapter 9

1. When I asked Elisebeth (EV) VanderWeil during a conference presentation about the idea of visionary literacy as a fresh peach and, concomitantly, the inevitable maggots in some of life's peaches, she replied by shrugging her shoulders and saying, "Maggots have protein."
2. See Alexie (2004).
3. According to Wikipedia, "Dadaism" is "a cultural movement that began in neutral Zurich, Switzerland, during World War I" and "primarily involved visual arts, literature (poetry, art manifestoes, art theory), theatre, and graphic design, which concentrated its anti war politic through a rejection of the prevailing standards in art through anti-art cultural works."
4. See Walker (2004).

References

Alexie, Sherman. 2004. Do not go gentle. In *The impossible will take a little while: A citizen's guide to hope in a time of fear,* ed. Paul R. Loeb, 163–168. New York: Basic Books.

Antrop-González, Rene, and Anthony De Jesús. 2006. Toward a theory of *critical care* in urban small school reform: Examining structures and pedagogies of caring in two Latino community-based schools. *Qualitative Studies in Education* 19 (4): 409–433.

Anyon, Jean. 2005. *Radical possibilities: Public policy, urban education, and a new social movement.* New York: Routledge.

———. 2006. What should count as educational research: Notes toward a new paradigm. In *Education research in the public interest: Social justice, action, and policy,* ed. Gloria Ladson-Billings and William F. Tate, 17–26. New York: Teachers College Press.

Apple, Michael W. 2000. *Official knowledge: Democratic education in a conservative age.* New York: Routledge.

———. 2001. *Educating the "right" way: Markets, standards, God, and inequality.* New York: RoutledgeFalmer.

Ashby, Ruth, and Deborah G. Ohrn. 1995. *Herstory: Women who changed the world.* New York: Penguin.

Avi. 1991. *Nothing but the truth: A documentary novel.* New York: Scholastic.

Ayers, William. 2006. Trudge toward freedom: Educational research in the public interest. In *Education research in the public interest: Social justice, action, and policy,* ed. Gloria Ladson-Billings and William F. Tate, 81–98. New York: Teachers College Press.

Banks, James A. 2006. Series foreword. In *Education research in the public interest: Social justice, action, and policy,* ed. Gloria Ladson-Billings and William F. Tate, ix–xiv. New York: Teachers College Press.

Barone, Thomas. 2006. Making educational history: Qualitative inquiry, artistry, and the public interest. In *Education research in the public interest: Social justice, action, and policy,* ed. Gloria Ladson-Billings and William F. Tate, 213–230. New York: Teachers College Press.

Bauer, Marion D., ed. 1994. *Am I blue?: Coming out from the silence.* New York: HarperCollins.

Bender-Slack, L., and M. P. Raupach. 2006. Teaching for social justice and teaching controversial issues: Are they one and the same? *Wisconsin Social Studies Journal* Spring: 33–37.

Berlak, Ann C. 2004. Confrontations and pedagogy: Cultural secrets, trauma, and emotion in antioppressive pedagogies. In *Democratic dialogue in education: Troubling speech, disturbing silence,* ed. Megan Boler, 123–144. New York: Peter Lang.

Bloom, Leslie. R. 1996. Stories of one's own: Nonunitary subjectivity in narrative representation. *Qualitative Inquiry* 2 (2): 176–197.

Boal, Augusto. 1979. *Theatre of the oppressed.* New York: Urizen Books.

Boler, Megan. 2004. All speech is not free: The ethics of "affirmative action pedagogy." In *Democratic dialogue in education: Troubling speech, disturbing silence,* ed. Megan Boler, 3–13. New York: Peter Lang.

Britzman, Deborah P. 1998. *Lost subjects, contested objects: Toward a psychoanalytic inquiry of learning.* Albany: State University of New York Press.

———. 2003. *Practice makes practice: A critical study of learning to teach, revised edition.* Albany: State University of New York Press.

Buehl, Doug. 2001. *Classroom strategies for interactive learning.* Newark, DE: International Reading Association.

Burbules, Nicholas. 2004. Introduction. In *Democratic dialogue in education: Troubling speech, disturbing silence,* ed. Megan Boler, xiii–xxxii. New York: Peter Lang.

Butin, Dan W. 2002. This ain't talk therapy: Problematizing and extending anti-oppressive education. *Educational Researcher* 31 (3): 14–16.

California Newsreel. 2003. The house we live in. Part three of *Race: The power of an illusion.* San Francisco.

Chodron, Pema. 2006. *Practicing peace in times of war.* Boston: Shambhala Publications, Inc.

CNN. 2006. Fifth girl dies after Amish school shooting. CNN News. www.cnn.com/2006/US/10/02/amish.shooting/index.html (accessed April 2007).

Collins, Patricia H. 2000. What's going on? Black feminist thought and the politics of postmodernism. In *Working the ruins: Feminist poststructural theory and methods in education,* ed. Elizabeth St. Pierre and Wanda S. Pillow, 41–73. New York: Routledge.

Cornbleth, Catherine, and Dexter Waugh. 1995. *The great speckled bird: Multicultural politics and education policymaking.* Mahwah, NJ: Lawrence Erlbaum.

Dance, L. Janelle. 2002. *Tough fronts: The impact of street culture on schooling.* New York: RoutledgeFalmer.

Darling-Hammond, Linda, and Milbrey McLaughlin. 1995. Policies that support professional development in an era of reform. *Phi Delta Kappan* 76 (8): 597–604.

Delpit, Lisa. 1995. *Other people's children: Cultural conflict in the classroom.* New York: New Press.

Dickinson, Emily. 1924. 115. In *The complete poems of Emily Dickinson,* ed. Martha D. Bianchi. Boston: Little, Brown, and Company.

———. 1936. 419. In *Unpublished poems of Emily Dickinson,* ed. Martha D. Bianchi and Alfred L. Hampson. Boston: Little, Brown, and Company.

Ehrenreich, Barbara. 2001. *Nickel and dimed: On (not) getting by in America.* New York: Henry Holt and Company.

Elias, John L. 1995. *Philosophy of education: Classical and contemporary.* Malabar, FL: Krieger Publishing Company.

Ellis, Carolyn. 2004. *The ethnographic I: A methodological novel about auto-ethnography.* Walnut Creek, CA: Altamira Press.

Ellsworth, Elizabeth. 1989. Why doesn't this feel empowering? Working through the repressive myths of critical pedagogy. *Harvard Educational Review* 59 (3): 297–324.

Emerson, Robert M., Rachel I. Fretz, and Linda L. Shaw. 1995. *Writing ethnographic fieldnotes.* Chicago: University of Chicago Press.

Finnessy, Patrick. 2007. Queer aporias: Straight teachers and a sexual minority curriculum. Paper presented at the annual meeting of the Center for Anti-Oppressive Education, January 12–14, in Chicago, IL.

Fontana, Andrea, and James H. Frey. (2000). The interview: From structured questions to negotiated text. In *Handbook of qualitative research, second edition,* ed. Norman K. Denzin and Yvonne S. Lincoln, 645–672. Thousand Oaks, CA: Sage Publications.

Fordham, Signithia. 1996. *Blacked out: Dilemmas of race, identity, and success at Capital High.* Chicago: University of Chicago Press.

Fraser, Nancy. 1997. *Justice interruptus: Critical reflections on the "postsocialist" condition.* New York: Routldege.

Freire, Paulo. 1970/1994. *Pedagogy of the oppressed.* New York: Continuum.

Freire, Paolo, and Donaldo Macedo. 1987. *Reading the word and the world.* South Hadley, MA: Bergin and Garvey.

Garrison, James. 2004. Ameliorating violence in dialogues across differences: The role of *eros* and *lógos*. In *Democratic dialogue in education: Troubling speech, disturbing silence,* ed. Megan Boler, 89–103. New York: Peter Lang.

Gee, James P. 1996. *Social linguistics and literacies: Ideology in discourses, second edition.* New York: RoutledgeFalmer.

Glodoski, Ron. 1998. *How to be a successful criminal: The real deal on crimes, drugs, and easy money.* Colorado Springs, CO: Turn Around Publishing.

Gorski, Paul C. 2007. Complicity with conservatism: The de-politicizing and re-politicizing of social justice education. Paper presented at the annual meeting of the Center for Anti-Oppressive Education, January 12–14, in Chicago, IL.

Grant, Carl A., and Vonzell Agosto. 2008. Social justice and teacher capacity in teacher education. In *Handbook of research on teacher education: Enduring questions in changing contexts, third edition,* ed. Marilyn Cochran-Smith, Sharon Feiman-Nemser, Kelly E. Demers, and John McIntyre, 175–200. Mahwah, NJ: Lawrence Erlbaum.

Greene, Maxine. 1995. *Releasing the imagination: Essays on education, the arts, and social change.* San Francisco: Jossey-Bass.

Grossman, Pamela, Sam Wineburg, and Stephen Woolworth. 2000. *What makes teacher community different from a gathering of teachers?* Seattle: University of Washington's Center for the Study of Teaching.

Grumet, Madeleine R. 1993. The play of meanings in the art of teaching. *Theory into Practice,* 32 (4): 204–209.

Gutmann, Amy. 1999. *Democratic Education.* Princeton, NJ: Princeton University Press.

Gutstein, Eric. 2006. *Reading and writing the world with mathematics: Toward a pedagogy of social justice.* New York: Routledge.

Haley, Alex. 1964. *The autobiography of Malcolm X: As told to Alex Haley.* New York: Ballantine Publishing Group.

Harding, Sandra. 1987. Conclusion: Epistemological questions. In *Feminism and methodology: Social science issues,* ed. Sandra Harding, 181–190. Bloomington: Indiana University Press.

Harris Interactive and GLSEN. 2005. *From teasing to torment: School climate in America, a survey of students and teachers.* New York: GLSEN.

Heath, Shirley B., and Milbrey H. McLaughlin. 1993. Building identities for inner-city youth. In *Identity and inner-city youth: Beyond ethnicity and gender,* ed. Shirley B. Heath and Milbrey H. McLaughlin, 1–12. New York: Teachers College Press.

Hess, Diana. 2004. Discussion in social studies: Is it worth the trouble? *Social Education* 68 (2): 151–155.

Hess, Diana, and Jeremy Stoddard. 2007. 9/11 and terrorism: "The ultimate teachable moment" in textbooks and supplemental curricula. *Social Education* 71 (5): 231–236.

Hibbing, John R., and Elizabeth Theiss-Morse. 2002. *Stealth democracy: Americans' beliefs about how government should work.* New York: Cambridge University Press.

Hollingsworth, Sandra. 1994. *Teacher research and urban literacy education: Lessons and conversations in a feminist key.* New York: Teachers College Press.

Hursh, David. 2006. Carry it on: Fighting the progressive education in neoliberal times. In *Education research in the public interest: Social justice, action, and policy,* ed. Gloria Ladson-Billings and William F. Tate, 46–63. New York: Teachers College Press.

Jensen, Derrick. 2004. *Listening to the land: Conversations about nature, culture, and eros.* White River Jct., VT: Chelsea Green Publishing.

Johnson, David W., and Roger. T. Johnson. 1995. *Creative controversy: Intellectual challenge in the classroom, third edition.* Edina, MN: Interaction Book Company.

Jordan, June. 1980. *Passion: New poems, 1977–1980.* Boston: Beacon Press.

Kendall, Marilyn, and Scott A. Murray. 2005. Tales of the unexpected: Patients' poetic accounts of the journey to a diagnosis of lung cancer: A prospective serial qualitative interview study. *Qualitative Inquiry* 11 (5): 733–751.

Kozol, Jonathan. 2005. Still separate, still unequal: America's educational apartheid. *Harper's Magazine* 311 (1864): 41–54.

———. 2007. NCLB and the poisonous essence of obsessive testing. Huffington Post. www.commondreams.org/archive/2007/09/13/3809/(accessed April 2008).

Kroft, Steve. 2006. Welcome to Hazleton: One mayor's controversial plan to deal with illegal immigration. CBS News. www.cbsnews.com/stories/2006/11/17/60minutes/main2195789.shtml (accessed October 2007).

Kumashiro, Kevin K. 1999. Supplementing normalcy and otherness: Queer Asian American men reflect on stereotypes, identity, and oppression. *Qualitative Studies in Education* 12 (5): 491–508.

———. 2002. *Troubling education: Queer activism and antioppressive pedagogy.* New York: RoutledgeFalmer.

———. 2008. *The seduction of common sense: How the right has framed the debate on America's schools.* New York: Teachers College Press.

Kunjufu, Jawanza. 2002. *Black students. Middle class teachers.* Chicago: African American Images.

Ladson-Billings, Gloria. 1994. *The dreamkeepers: Successful teachers of African American children.* San Francisco: Jossey-Bass.

———. 1995. Toward a theory of culturally relevant pedagogy. *American Educational Research Journal* 40 (2): 465–491.

———. 2000. Racialized discourses and ethnic epistemologies. In *Handbook of qualitative research, second edition,* ed. Norman K. Denzin and Yvonne S. Lincoln, 257–278. Thousand Oaks, CA: Sage Publications, Inc.

Ladwig, James G. 1991. Is collaborative research exploitative? *Educational Theory* 41 (2): 111–120.

Lamott, Anne. 2005. *Plan B: Further thoughts on faith.* New York: Riverhead Books.

Lareau, Annette. 2003. *Unequal childhoods: Class, race, and family life.* Berkeley: University of California Press.

Lawrence-Lightfoot, Sara, and Jessica H. Davis. 1997. *The art and science of portraiture.* San Francisco: Jossey-Bass.

Leonardo, Zeus. 2004. Critical social theory and transformative knowledge: The functions of criticism in quality education. *Educational Researcher* 33 (6): 11–18.

Lightfoot, Sarah L. 1983. *The good high school: Portraits of character and culture.* New York: Basic Books.

Lipman, Pauline. 2004. *High stakes education: Inequality, globalization and urban school reform.* New York: Routledge.

Loeb, Paul R., ed. 2004. *The impossible will take a little while: A citizen's guide to hope in a time of fear.* New York: Basic Books.

Lopez, Nancy. 2003. *Hopeful girls, troubled boys: Race and gender disparity in urban education.* New York: Routledge.

Lowe, Robert. 2007. Backpedaling toward Plessy. *Rethinking Schools* 22 (1): 14–17.

Lynch, Kathleen, and John Baker. 2005. Equality in education: An equality of condition perspective. *Theory and Research in Education* 3 (2): 131–164.

Maguire, Patricia. 1993. Challenges, contradictions, and celebrations: Attempting participatory research as a doctoral student. In *Voices of change: Participatory research in the United States and Canada,* ed. Peter Park, Mary Brydon-Miller, Bud Hall, and Ted Jackson, 157–176. Westport, CT: Bergin & Garvey.

Manes, Christopher. 1990. *Green rage: Radical environmentalism and the unmaking of civilization.* Waltham, MA: Little, Brown and Company.

Max-Neef, Manfred, Antonio Elizalde, and Martin Hopenhayn. 1991. *Human scale development: Conception, application and further reflections.* New York: Apex Press.

Mayo, Cris. 2004. The tolerance that dare not speak its name. In *Democratic dialogue in education: Troubling speech, disturbing silence,* ed. Megan Boler, 33–47. New York: Peter Lang.

McCready, Lance T. 2005. Some challenges facing queer youth programs in urban high schools: Racial segregation and denormalizing whiteness. In *Gay, lesbian, and transgender issues in education: Programs, policies, and practices,* ed. James T. Sears, 185–197. New York: Harrington Park Press.

McDaniel, Janet E., Francisco A. Ríos, Juan Necochea, Laura P. Stowell, and Charlotte F. Kritzer. 2001. Envisioning the arc of social justice in middle schools. *Middle School Journal* 33 (1): 28–34.

McNeil, Linda M. 2000a. *Contradictions of school reform: Educational costs of standardized testing.* New York: Routledge.

———. 2000b. Faking equity: High stakes testing and Latino youth. *Phi Delta Kappan* 81 (10): 728–734.

Meiners, Erica. R. 2007. *Right to be hostile: Schools, prisons, and the making of public enemies.* New York: Routledge.

Meiners, Erica, and Therese Quinn. 2007. How real does it get? *AREA Chicago* 5: 28.

Michelli, Nicholas M. 2005. Education for democracy: What can it be? In *Teacher education for democracy and social education,* ed. Nicholas M. Michelli and David L. Keiser, 3–30. New York: Routledge.

Michelli, Nicholas M., and David L. Keiser. 2005. Introduction: Teacher education for democracy and social justice. In *Teacher education for democracy and social education,* ed. Nicholas M. Michelli and David L. Keiser, xvii–xxv. New York: Routledge.

Mikaelsen, Ben. 2001. *Touching Spirit Bear.* New York: HarperCollins.

Mun Wah, Lee. 1994. *The Color of Fear.* Berkeley, CA: StirFry Seminars.

Myers, Walter D. 1991. *Fallen Angels.* New York: Scholastic.

———. 1999. *Monster.* New York: HarperCollins.

Naylor, Brian. 2007. Bill giving children path to citizenship blocked. National Public Radio. www.npr.org/templates/story/story.php?storyId=15604139 (accessed December 2007).

Newkirk, Reggie, and Nathan Rutstein. 2000. *Racial healing: The institutes for the healing of racism.* Albion, MI: National Resource Center for the Healing of Racism.

Nhat Hanh, Thich. 1992. *Peace is every step: The path of mindfulness in everyday life.* New York: Bantam Books.

Nichols, Sharon L., Gene V. Glass, and David C. Berliner. 2005. *High-stakes testing and student achievement: Problems for the No Child Left Behind Act.* Tempe, AZ: Education Policy Studies Laboratory.

Noddings, Nel. 1984. *Caring: A feminine approach to ethics and moral education.* Berkeley: University of California Press.

Nussbaum, Martha C. 2004. *Hiding from humanity: Disgust, shame, and the law.* Princeton, NJ: Princeton University Press.

Nystrand, Martin. 1997. *Opening dialogue: Understanding the dynamics of language learning in the English classroom.* New York: Teachers College Press.

Obidah, Jennifer E., and Karen M. Teel. 2001. *Because of the kids: Facing racial and cultural differences in schools.* New York: Teachers College Press.

Olneck, Michael. 2000. Can multicultural education change what counts as cultural capital? *American Educational Research Journal* 37 (2): 317–348.

Orfield, Gary, Erica D. Frankenberg, and Chungmei Lee. 2002. The resurgence of school segregation. *Educational Leadership* 60 (4): 16–20.

Paley, Vivian G. 1992. *You can't say you can't play.* Cambridge, MA: Harvard University Press.

Palmer, Parker J. 1998. *The courage to teach: Exploring the inner landscape of a teacher's life.* San Francisco: Jossey-Bass.

Parker, Walter C. 2003. *Teaching democracy: Unity and diversity in public life.* New York: Teachers College Press.

———. 2006. Public discourses in schools: Purposes, problems, possibilities. *Educational Researcher* 35 (8): 11–18.

Pattillo, Mary. 2007. *Black on the block: The politics of race and class in the city.* Chicago: University of Chicago Press.

Payne, Ruby K. 2001. *A framework for understanding poverty.* Highlands, TX: Aha! Process, Inc.

Popkewitz, Thomas S. 1998. *Struggling for the soul: The politics of schooling and the construction of the teacher.* New York: Teachers College Press.

———. 2006. Hopes of progress and fears of the dangerous: Research, cultural theses, and planning different human kinds. In *Education research in the public interest: Social justice, action, and policy,* ed. Gloria Ladson-Billings and William F. Tate, 119–140. New York: Teachers College Press.

Ray, Brian D. 2005. *Worldwide guide to homeschooling: Facts and stats on the benefits of home school, 2005–2006.* Nashville, TN: B&H Publishing Group.

Reich, Rob. 2002. *Bridging liberalism and multiculturalism in American education.* Chicago: University of Chicago Press.

Richardson, Laurel. 2000. Writing: A method of inquiry. In *Handbook of qualitative research,* ed. Norman K. Denzin and Yvonne S. Lincoln, 923–948. Thousand Oaks, CA: Sage Publications, Inc.

Scott, Joan W. 2005. Feminism's history. *Journal of Women's History* 16 (2): 10–29.

Segall, Avner. 2002. *Disturbing practice: Reading teacher education as text.* New York: Peter Lang.

Shulman, Lee S. 1986. Those who understand: Knowledge growth in teaching. *Educational Researcher* 15 (2): 4–14.

Smith, Linda T. 1999. *Decolonizing methodologies: Research and indigenous peoples.* New York: Zed Books.

Spiegelman, Art. 1986. *Maus I: A survivor's tale: My father bleeds history.* New York: Pantheon.

St. Pierre, Elizabeth A. 2000. Poststructural feminism in education: An overview. *Qualitative Studies in Education* 13 (5): 477–515.

Stovall, David. 2006. Urban poetics: Poetry, social justice and critical pedagogy in education. *Urban Review* 38 (1): 63–80.

Suarez-Orozco, Marcelo M. 2001. Globalization, immigration, and education: The research agenda. *Harvard Educational Review* 71 (3): 345–365.

Tannen, Deborah. 1986. *That's not what I meant: How conversational style makes or breaks relationships.* New York: Ballantine Books.

Tate, William F. 1997. Critical race theory and education: History, theory, and implications. *Review of Research in Education* 22: 195–247.

———. 2006. Afterword: In the public interest. In *Education research in the public interest: Social justice, action, and policy,* ed. Gloria Ladson-Billings and William F. Tate, 247–260. New York: Teachers College Press.

Tirrell-Corbin, Christy, and David H. Cooper. 2008. Dewey the "D" in PDS. Paper presented at the annual meeting of the American Educational Research Association, March 24–28, in New York, NY.

Tochon, Francois V. 1999. *Video study groups: For education, professional development, and change.* Madison, WI: Atwood Publishing.

Tyack, David, and Larry Cuban. 1995. *Tinkering toward utopia: A century of public school reform.* Cambridge, MA: Harvard University Press.

Tye, Barbara B. 2000. *Hard truths: Uncovering the deep structure of schooling.* New York: Teachers College Press.

U.S. Census Bureau. Poverty: 2005 highlights. www.census.gov/hhes/www/poverty/poverty05/pov05hi.html (accessed February 2007).

Valenzuela, Angela. 1999. *Subtractive schooling: U.S.-Mexican youth and the politics of caring.* Albany: SUNY Press.

VanderWeil, Elisebeth. 2007. Not enough chairs: The art of hosting learning. Paper presented at the annual meeting of the Center for Anti-Oppressive Education, January 12–14, in Chicago, IL.

Villegas, Ana M., and Tamara Lucas. 1998. *Educating culturally responsive teachers: A coherent approach.* Albany: SUNY Press.

Walker, Alice. 2004. Only justice can stop a curse. In *The impossible will take a little while: A citizen's guide to hope in a time of fear,* ed. Paul R. Loeb, 361–367. New York: Basic Books.

West, Cornell. 2004. *Democracy matters: Winning the fight against imperialism.* New York: Penguin Press.

West, Peg F. 1984. *Protective behaviors: Anti-victim training for children, adolescents, and adults.* Madison, WI: Protective Behaviors, Inc.

Westheimer, Joel, and Joseph Kahne. 2002. Educating the "good" citizen: The politics of school-based democracy education programs. Paper presented at the annual meeting of the American Political Science Association, Aug. 29–Sept. 1, in Boston, MA.

Wikipedia. Dadaism. www.en.wikipedia.org/wiki/Dadaism (accessed March 2007).

Wilson, Timothy. 2002. *Strangers to ourselves: Discovering the adaptive unconscious.* Cambridge, MA: Harvard University Press.

Wynter, Sylvia. 2006. On how we mistook the map for the territory, and re-imprisoned ourselves in our unbearable wrongness of being, of *Désêtre*: Black studies toward the human project. In *Not only the master's tools: African-American studies in theory and practice,* ed. Lewis R. Gordon and Jane A. Gordon, 107–169. Boulder, CO: Paradigm Publishers.

Yoshino, Kenji. 2006. *Covering: The hidden assault on our civil rights.* New York: Random House.

Young, Iris M. 1990. *Justice and the politics of difference.* Princeton, NJ: Princeton University Press.

Younger, Mike R., and Molly Warrington. 2006. Would Harry and Hermione have done better in single-sex classes? A review of single-sex teaching in coeducational secondary schools in the United Kingdom. *American Educational Research Journal* 43 (4): 579–620.

Zeichner, Kenneth M., and Susan E. Noffke. 2001. Practitioner research. In *Handbook of research on teaching,* ed. Virginia Richardson, 298–330. Washington, DC: American Educational Research Association.

Index

in the life of, 81–83; on discussion in democratic classroom, 132–135; meeting, 80–81; in hope discussion, 152–153; illegal immigration classroom discussion of, 139–145; as invisible student, 93; mathematics position returned to by, 92; path to teaching of, 83–85; political views not shared by, 141–142; racialized conflict and, 89–93; in "Shutting All the Doors" dialogue, 65–69; study group's meaning to, 164–165; study skills class modified by, 81–82; teaching epiphany of, 85; teaching philosophy of, 93–95; on transforming authoritarian to connected culture, 98–104; trust in, 89; weekly reading goals of, 82

King, Coretta Scott, 126
knowledge construction, 30, 146
knowledge organization, 30f
Kumashiro, Kevin, 2

labels, power of, 121, 154
laborers, 29
Ladson-Billing, Gloria, 70
Lakeside School, 114, 132; admission criteria at, 121; African-Americans lacking at, 122; central mission statement at, 124–125; democratic education at, 120, 123; parental involvement in, 123–124; private status shielding, 138; as progressive, 120–121; scholarships for, 121; student demographics at, 121–122, 138
language, power of, 141
Lareau, Annette, 126
Latin-American history, 56
leadership roles, 21
learning objects, 116–117
lessons, scaffolding, 14
LGBTQ individuals, 48, 72–74, 88, 137
Libya, bombing of, 54
life as stick metaphor, 155–156

life lessons, 104
listening across difference strategies, 143
Listening to the Land (Jensen), 52
literacy: importance of contextualizing, 162–163; improving, 19; model emerging of, 170; not limited to reading and writing, 5; tutor, 17. *See also* critical literacy; democratic literacy; functional literacy; relational literacy; visionary literacy
Loeb, Paul, 51, 67
long-term planning, 32
Lopez, Nancy, 40
low-paid service jobs, 29
Lucas, Tamara, 39
Lynch, Kathleen, 96

magic words, 10–12
Mandela, Nelson, 69
Mane, Christopher, 52–53
Margaret, 5, 163; accusations of Latinos favored by, 107; caring behaviors of, 105–106; in context discussion, 160–161; derisive comments in classroom of, 73; on discussion in democratic classroom, 131–135; fears identified by, 144; meeting with, 12–14; frustration of, 16, 163–164; life as stick metaphor of, 155–156; magic words of, 10–12; path to teaching of, 16–17; poem by, 18; political views not shared by, 141–142; restrictions on, 139; shifting from authoritarian figure to facilitator, 136; in "Shutting All the Doors" dialogue, 63–69; as surrogate parent, 99–100; teaching philosophy of, 22–27; on transforming authoritarian to connected culture, 99–104. *See also* Socratic Circles
McDaniel, Jack, 37
mentoring: students, 44; of young teachers, 34
middle-class parents, 126
Mikaelsen, Ben, 30, 154–155, 172n1

About the Author

Connie E. North received her doctorate from the Departments of Curriculum and Instruction and Educational Policy Studies at the University of Wisconsin–Madison. She specializes in teacher and antioppressive education and is an assistant professor in the Department of Curriculum and Instruction at the University of Maryland, College Park.